Canadians at War

Also by SUSAN EVANS SHAW

*Canadians at War: Vol. 1, A Guide to the Battlefields
and Memorials of World War I*
Photography by Jean Crankshaw (2012)

*Heritage Treasures: The Historic Homes of Ancaster,
Burlington, Dundas, East Flamborough, Hamilton,
Stoney Creek and Waterdown*,
with Jean Crankshaw (2004)

*My Darling Girl: Wartime Letters of
James Lloyd Evans 1914-1918* (1999)

Canadians at War

VOL. 2, A GUIDE TO THE BATTLEFIELDS AND MEMORIALS OF WORLD WAR II

Susan Evans Shaw

Edited by Barry Norris.
Cover and page design by Julie Scriver.
Cover photographs by Susan Evans Shaw, unless otherwise noted.
Front cover, clockwise from top: Juno Beach Centre sculpture, *Remembrance and Renewal*, created by Canadian sculptor Colin Gibson, west-facing aspect, Courseulles-sur-Mer, Normandy (photo by Janice Jackson); Veterans at parade (photo by Janice Jackson); Commonwealth Air Force Memorial, Ottawa; Hong Kong Veterans Memorial Wall, Ottawa; La Cambe German Cemetery, near Bayeux, Normandy.
Back cover, left to right: Brookwood Memorial, Surrey; Plaque to the Queen's Own Rifles of Canada, Bernières-sur-Mer, Normandy; Juno Beach Centre, western aspect (photo by Janice Jackson).

Library and Archives Canada Cataloguing in Publication

Evans Shaw, Susan, 1944-, author
Canadians at war. Vol. 2, A guide to the battlefields and memorials of World War II / Susan Evans Shaw.

Includes bibliographical references and index.
Issued in print and electronic formats.
ISBN 978-0-86492-444-5 (pbk.). — ISBN 978-0-86492-720-0 (pdf)

1. Canada. Canadian Armed Forces — History — World War, 1939-1945.
2. World War, 1939-1945 — Canada. 3. World War, 1939-1945 — Battlefields — Guidebooks. 4. World War, 1939-1945 — Monuments — Guidebooks. I. Title.

D768.15.E93 2014   940.54'1271   C2013-907628-X
                                      C2013-907629-8

Goose Lane Editions acknowledges the generous support of the Canada Council for the Arts, the Government of Canada through the Canada Book Fund (CBF), and the Government of New Brunswick through the Department of Tourism, Heritage and Culture.

Goose Lane Editions
500 Beaverbrook Court, Suite 330
Fredericton, New Brunswick
CANADA E3B 5X4
www.gooselane.com

RECYCLED
Paper made from
recycled material
FSC® C103567

All deserve tribute and win their place in the Pantheon.
— Douglas LePan, *Macalister, or Dying in the Dark* (1995)

To Sam
and in memory of Denis, David, and Terry

Contents

Preface

I have little direct connection to World War II, unlike World War I, in which my grandfather, James Lloyd Evans, was killed in 1918. As the son of a soldier who died in the war, my Uncle Frank, a very promising student, learned he was eligible for an Imperial Order of the Daughters of the Empire (IODE) university scholarship. He enrolled at the University of Manitoba and became the first in the family and the first in the village of Miniota, Manitoba, to attend university. My father, Eric, eight years younger than Frank, eventually followed his brother to the University of Manitoba. Frank Evans became a civil engineer and Eric Evans, a geologist. For the duration of World War II both pursued their professions where they were needed in Canada. Having lost her husband in the Great War, my grandmother was more than relieved at not having to face another heartbreaking loss. Tragedy struck nonetheless. Frank, now married and the father of two daughters, died of an infection from an insect bite in 1943 while working at Rocky Mountain House, Alberta. Limited supplies of the recently discovered penicillin were reserved for the Allied military.

My mother, Diana Peacock, an only child, did have a brush with a wartime casualty—Frank Pickersgill. They met in 1934 as undergraduates at the University of Manitoba. Frank graduated in 1936 and in the fall left Winnipeg to do his master's degree at the University of Toronto. Diana remained in Winnipeg and struggled to complete a Home Economics degree for which she had little aptitude. My mother and Frank met one last time, in 1938, at a train station in either Toronto or Ottawa. She was on her way to intern as a dietician at Ottawa Civic Hospital and he was heading to Montreal to board a ship for Paris, where he planned to continue his studies.

Frank would never return to Canada. In Paris, he met with a coterie of friends, among them Kay Moore from the University of Manitoba and Mary Mundle from Scotland. When Paris fell to Hitler's army, Kay and Mary made their escape but Frank remained behind in France. Eventually he was caught and imprisoned for eighteen months at St-Denis until he and another prisoner managed an escape. They fled to Vichy France and finally to Lisbon, where, after a few tedious months, Frank managed to get a place on a flight to England in October 1942.

Once back in England, Frank resolved to return to France to join the Resistance and the fight to free Europe from German occupation. Being a fluent speaker of French, Frank was recruited by the Special Operations Executive (SOE). For the next year he trained in espionage, an intensive course that included the art of silent killing. His friends from Paris, Kay and Mary, were now living in Knightsbridge, sharing a house with Alison Grant. Mary and Kay worked in SOE in the section that trained, supplied, and transported agents for the intelligence wing of Charles de Gaulle's Free French Forces. Alison worked for Military Intelligence. Frank and his fellow trainee, Ken Macalister from Guelph, made their home away from home on the third floor of the same Knightsbridge house during rest periods from training.

In June 1943, Ken and Frank parachuted by night into occupied France unaware that the Germans had infiltrated the resistance network. Within a week they were captured as the Germans swept up agents one by one and imprisoned them in concentration camps outside Paris. As the Allies approached Paris in August 1944, after months of torture and near starvation, a selection from the resistance group, including Frank and Ken, was transported to Buchenwald. There, on September 14, 1944, the SS executed Frank, Ken, and eleven others, stringing them up with piano wire on meat hooks so that each man strangled to death. They then heaved the bodies down, piled them on an electric lift, and sent them upstairs to the coke-fired crematorium.[1]

After the war, Alison returned to Canada and married George

Ignatieff. According to her son, Michael, "she never doubted that Frank had done the right thing or that she or anyone else could have stopped him from doing what he had to do. She taught her children to revere Frank's example."[2]

My mother in Canada knew nothing of what happened to Frank after they parted. In 1948, Frank's older brother, J.W. Pickersgill, privately published *The Letters of Frank Pickersgill, 1934-1943* as a limited edition. Diana, now married to Eric Evans and the mother of two daughters, obtained a copy into which she pasted her nameplate, the only book she ever so marked. I found the book among her papers after she died, which is how I came to piece together a history starting with her oft-repeated memories of Frank Pickersgill.

Movies about World War II, mostly American and British, tend to present the war as non-stop suspenseful action. In fact, for the army, that was hardly the case. Hitler moved so swiftly through Europe that the British never got a chance to establish a Western Front as they had in 1914. Instead, they were forced back to the temporary toehold of Dunkirk, which ended in an ignominious retreat. Until the fiasco of Dieppe in 1942, then the brilliantly successful D-Day invasion in 1944, for Canadians the war in Northwest Europe meant training for the battles to come and defending British shores from possible invasion. Underground resistance in the early years of the war combined with the naval battles of the North Atlantic and battles in the air over Britain and Western Europe saw Britain and its allies locked in a mammoth struggle, if not to dislodge the Germans from conquered territory, then at least to impede the spread of Nazi power. This stalemate continued until the Allied landings in Sicily in 1943, when at last the pushback of the German Army began. What follows is the story of the part Canada played.

Canadians at War: Vol.1, A Guide to the Battlefields and Memorials of World War I would not be complete without a companion volume on World War II to round out a compact history and travel guide to the two great wars of the twentieth century. According to reviews of the earlier work, a pocket-sized history and guide to the battlefields of World War I was long overdue, and the same applies to the war that followed in 1939. In fact, the two wars, with the twenty-one year-interlude, could be considered a Thirty Years' War on a far vaster scale than the war of that name almost exactly three hundred years earlier. However, such a discussion is beyond the scope of this work.

The second world war posed an enormous logistical problem for the author and will do so for the traveller as the Canadians served in such widespread areas—Britain, Hong Kong, Dieppe, Italy, and Northwest Europe. Accordingly, I chose to divide this guide in six parts, one part for the pre-war and Phoney War period, four separate parts to cover the

Four veterans of Dieppe attending the 70th anniversary memorial service, August 2012, at the Dieppe Memorial in Hamilton, Ontario. Left to right: Stan Darch RHLI, Gordon McPartlin RHLI, Jack MacFarland RHLI, Fred Nicholls RHLI.
(Susan Evans Shaw)

different areas and battles, and a final section to cover the odds and ends of the war.

Interest is mounting as World War II passes beyond living memory and into recorded history. Descendants of those who served and those who lived through the tension and chaos of the years 1939-1945 want to see for themselves the remnants and memorials. That they place importance on such visits is a tribute to the legacy of the Canadian men and women caught up in the maelstrom of war, to those who died and to those who returned.

On a practical note: I've tried to give as complete directions as possible to the individual cemeteries and memorials. Unfortunately, information on public transit is not always available and in many cases, particularly in Italy, the best option is a taxi from the nearest centre if the distance from the train station is too great to cover on foot. Inquiries within the country about local transit may prove helpful.

Introduction

Canada is an unmilitary community. Warlike her people have
often been forced to be; military they have never been.[1]

With the return of peace in 1919, Canadians settled into their ordinary
lives. The large gaps left by those who never came back from the
battlefields could never be filled; nevertheless, it was a time of rest and
recovery. As far as Canadians were concerned, "the war to end all wars" was
exactly that. The Great War would have no long-term effect on Canada's
military policy.[2] The four divisions that served so admirably at Vimy, Hill
70, Amiens, and beyond were disbanded, leaving a mere skeleton force.

General Sir Arthur Currie, commander of the 1st Division at Vimy
Ridge and later the first Canadian appointed to serve as Army Corps
commander of the Canadian Expeditionary Force, returned to Canada
in 1919 with little fanfare and a lukewarm public reception.[3] Unlike the
other senior generals of the British Empire, General Currie received no
thanks from his government,[4] nor did Prime Minister Robert Borden's
cabinet vote him a cash reward.[5] Instead, in the House of Commons,
safe from charges of libel, Sam Hughes, former Minister of Militia, rose
to make a speech accusing General Currie of needlessly wasting men's
lives at Mons in the final hours of the war.

Eight years passed before Currie could clear his name. In June 1927,
on the occasion of the installation of a memorial plaque to the Canadians
at Mons, the Port Hope *Evening Star* published an editorial that reiterated
Hughes's accusation of men's lives wasted. Currie sued. He won the case
but the restoration of his reputation came at the price of his health. On
November 30, 1933, General Sir Arthur Currie died, age fifty-eight, in

Montreal, where he had served as principal of McGill University since 1920. This time, Canada honoured Currie as he so rightly deserved. He was given a state funeral more elaborate even than those for Sir John A. Macdonald or Sir Wilfrid Laurier. Crowds lined the streets of Montreal to witness the funeral cortège with Currie's flag-draped casket transported on a horse-drawn gun carriage. Sir Arthur's own wartime charger, Brock, was by now too old and frail to take part in the procession.[6] In his place, two handlers on foot led a magnificent young charger carrying the traditional empty saddle, boots reversed in the stirrups. Behind walked Currie's son Garner, Currie's brother John, the prime minister, the governor general, dignitaries both Canadian and foreign, civil and military. The CBC carried an unprecedented live coast-to-coast radio broadcast of the proceedings.[7] Eighteen months later and seventeen years after the victory at Mons, the Parliament of Canada awarded Currie's estate fifty thousand dollars in recognition of the general's service to the nation during the Great War.[8]

The year of Currie's death, 1933, also marked the rise to power of the National Socialist German Workers' Party (the Nazi Party) and the appointment, by President Paul von Hindenburg, of Adolf Hitler as Chancellor of Germany. Canada took little notice. In 1937, while overseas for the coronation of King George VI, Prime Minister William Lyon Mackenzie King met with Hitler in Berlin. He expressed admiration for

the man, finding in Hitler a kindred interest in mysticism, although he found Nazism repugnant.[9]

But even as the power and influence of Hitler's Third Reich grew, Canadians remained complacent. From the Plains of Abraham to the fields of Flanders, no

W.L. Mackenzie King, left, at the opening of the All-German Sports Competitions, Berlin, Germany, June 1937.
(Presse-Bild-Zentrale / Library and Archives Canada, PA-119007 / Wikimedia Commons / Public Domain)

battle fought ever convinced Canadians there was any connection between the nation's welfare and the state of its military preparations.[10] The fine Canadian Expeditionary Force of 425,000 men and women that served overseas from 1914 to 1918[11] had been reduced by 1937 to a paltry permanent force of fewer than ten thousand men under arms. The military machine had been dismantled, defence forces were negligible, and their equipment had become obsolete.[12]

Meanwhile, the events that were to lead to the outbreak of a second world war relentlessly unfolded. In defiance of the Versailles and Locarno treaties, Hitler reoccupied and rearmed the Rhineland in March 1936.[13] Next, he set his sights on Austria to further his plan of expansion and uniting the German-speaking peoples of Europe. On March 13, 1938, the German Army marched over the border to Linz and the *Anschluss*, the incorporation of Austria into the Greater German Reich, began.[14] Hitler was allowed to take possession of the Sudetenland, a region of Czechoslovakia inhabited mostly by German-speaking people. Then, on March 20, 1939, Hitler seized the rest of Czechoslovakia. Widespread public indignation in Britain and France was echoed in Canada. Hearing no suggestion of liberating Czechoslovakia and aware of no direct threat to Britain of an invasion, Mackenzie King declared there was no reason to despair of peace. Then, to his chagrin, Britain and France guaranteed the integrity of Poland.[15]

The possibility of Britain's going to war—a war in which Canada would undoubtedly take part—became a certainty when the signing of a non-aggression pact between Hitler and Stalin made inevitable an attack on Poland. Before a shot had been fired anywhere in actual combat, the Canadian government made a first step toward readiness for war by bringing the War Measures Act into force by proclamation.[16] Then, at the beginning of September, Parliament was called into session, and the army was placed on alert. On Sunday, September 3, 1939, France and Britain declared war on Germany. Mackenzie King announced that when Parliament met on September 7, the government would recommend that Canada go to war at Britain's side.

The vote was called on Saturday evening and the result was virtually unanimous.[17] On Sunday, September 10, King George VI announced that, by a decision of the Canadian Parliament, Canada was at war with Germany.

PART I

The Eve of War

The idea of once again raising great expeditionary forces to fight in France terrified [Mackenzie] King, to such an extent that he penned "a deep sadness" at the prospect of the 1st Canadian Division moving into a "fiery furnace to be devoured whole." Heavy casualties might easily trigger conscription — a policy decision that had divided the country during the First World War.[1]

Twenty eventful years had elapsed since the end of the Great War, yet that conflict continued to cast a long shadow. Rather than face the likelihood of another long and costly war, the Canadian public preferred to turn a blind eye toward events in Europe. Understandably, a general resistance to rearming prevailed. Memory of the annihilation of sixty thousand young men in "the war to end all wars" remained too fresh; a renewal of that struggle had no appeal.

Canadians so vehemently rejected the idea of military rearmament that remarkably little preparation had been made, especially considering the scale of the coming emergency.[2] Canada had no armament industry to speak of and relied on Britain for military supplies. Now with war imminent, shipments to Canada dwindled to almost nothing. The first years of the war would have to be spent developing industries to produce small arms, bombs, and ammunition. Full production would not be attained until 1943. Meanwhile, troops trained at home, clad in musty uniforms resurrected from storage where they had been kept since 1918, using obsolete World War I equipment. On the plus side, Canada's well-developed auto industry enabled rapid conversion to production of mechanical transport.

Canada's Active Service Force consisted of original units of the Canadian Militia, wearing badges and the titles of long familiar regiments, adhering to inherited traditions and *esprit de corps* that formed part of Canadian history. These made up the service battalions of the militia regiments.[3] Recruiters urgently sought permanent force personnel to fill the roles of staff officers and instructors to train inexperienced volunteers, and among the first to join were veterans of the Canadian Expeditionary Force of 1914-1918, their number restricted only by medical standards and age limit. Most provinces responded well to the call, even in the absence of the jingoism and war excitement that had been evident in 1914. Support for French-speaking units turned out to be surprisingly high, while largely rural Saskatchewan, with its sizeable foreign-born population and approaching harvest season, proved to be the most sluggish.

The 1st Division shipped to England in December 1939 with the clear understanding that Canadian units would not be incorporated into the British Army but would remain together under Canadian command. Then, alarmed by Germany's rapid conquest of Norway, Denmark, Belgium, the Netherlands, and France in the spring and summer of 1940, Prime Minister Mackenzie King announced the formation of a Canadian Corps to serve in Europe. Ranks of all divisions, including officers and nursing sisters, filled without difficulty. In the period from May to August 1940, more than eighty-five thousand men and women joined the Canadian Active Service Force.[4] Eventually over 1.1 million men and women would serve in five divisions of the Canadian Forces—four divisions in Northwest Europe and one division in Italy.[5]

To encourage mobilization, Canada needed an image of a strong war leader, like Sir Arthur Currie had been in the earlier conflict. Mackenzie King, small of stature, tubby, and an uninspiring speaker, could not fill that role, so the public and press turned to Major-General A.G.M. (Andy) McNaughton, who had served under Currie in World War I and now became the first commander of the Canadian Corps. McNaughton's picture appeared on newspaper front pages, on posters, in the newsreels, and on magazine covers. He had a commanding presence and, for a time, was tipped as the probable commander of all Allied Forces for the Second Front.[6]

The Canadian Army Overseas

> Because of [Canadian Lieutenant-General H.D.G.] Crerar's dearth of training knowledge, [British general Bernard Law] Montgomery bore a great deal of responsibility for the training of Canadian formation commanders from regiment to division. . . . Montgomery declared with utter conviction: "Commanders and staff officers at any level who couldn't stand the strain, or who got tired, were to be weeded out and replaced — ruthlessly."[7]

As the war proceeded, it became evident that modern conditions required younger men in command of troops. At the outset of war in 1939, Canada possessed a considerable body of competent officers, but all those with the rank of lieutenant-colonel and above had seen service in 1914-1918. Some kept abreast of current military thought and availed themselves of command and staff instruction; others remained fixed on the military mores of the earlier war. In actual battle, the problem of selecting officers tends to solve itself, but for the Canadian Army during the long period of inactivity, the selection of officers involved a certain amount of instinct and guesswork in deciding those most competent to lead.[8] Some fulfilled their promise but others gave way to replacements.

McNaughton faced the unpleasant task of weeding out the unsuitable, but the principal housecleaning was carried out by British general Bernard Montgomery. With cold efficiency he dispatched home to Canada any senior officer who did not meet his exacting standards. A general who was to lead his troops into battle, particularly a cross-Channel invasion, had to demonstrate the skills of command in a modern army. Men's lives were at stake, and too many of the older generation could not break free from the conventions of trench warfare. By January 1944, most brigade commanders were below the age of thirty-five and most battalion commanders were under thirty.[9] Professional and business men in civilian life, often well educated and accustomed to direction of large enterprises, they took naturally and effectively to military command.

Beginnings

A Canadian regiment was composed of roughly nine hundred men and officers. There were four rifle companies, each consisting of three platoons; each platoon composed of three sections of ten men led by a corporal. These companies were called Able, Baker, Charlie and Dog, and they were the striking force, the reason for the Regiment's existence. Their sole function was fighting, and all their training was devoted to this end. The infantry soldier was required to be proficient in the handling of such weapons as his rifle and bayonet, the Bren light machine gun; the two-inch mortar; the .55 anti-tank rifle (and later the anti-tank projector); the Thompson submachine gun; the Sten [gun] and five varieties of hand grenades. . . . Each man had to be carefully versed in elementary tactics, in battle drills, in map reading, in field craft; in co-operation with other arms such as tanks, artillery, and the air force; in gas defence; in the rudiments of military law, field hygiene, patrol techniques, enemy methods and equipment, and a score of other vital subjects.[10]

At the time of their arrival in Britain, soldiers of the Canadian 1st Division had attained only the most elementary standard of preparation. Half the men had no military schooling or experience whatsoever. Installed in the frigid and antiquated barrack blocks at Aldershot in early January 1940, the men underwent rigorous drilling based on the military handbook, *Training Instruction No. 1*. Initially the emphasis was on musketry, including machine guns, but as Bren guns were in short supply the men had to learn using obsolete Lewis guns. Officers in training got special attention that included instruction in map and sand-table exercises as well as the fundamental principles of attack, defence, and commanding troops. In the matter of uniforms, kilts were eliminated from the Highland regiments. Bearing in mind the effect of blistering gases on unprotected skin in World War I, the Minister of National Defence decreed that battledress only was to be worn.[11] The "Ladies from Hell" would not appear in this new war.

Advanced training began in April 1940. Basing their instruction strategy on World War I drill and the 1918 *Pamphlet of Field Engineering*, officers had the troops spend their time in the miles of trench systems constructed for the purpose on Salisbury Plain. There they rehearsed outdated procedures such as patrolling, raiding, standing-to, and improving defences,[12] most of which were shown to be useless after the Germans swept across Europe in tanks. For high-spirited young Canadians eager to see action, the tedium of the first two years of barracks life and routine training told on morale, and was reflected in the number of men disciplined for being absent without leave.[13] The introduction of battle drill in 1941, a method of practising small unit tactics, provided the biggest lift to the tedium of the wait in England. Drill raised morale and transformed the training of troops.[14]

Initially, with the probability of invasion and a fight in the English countryside, the Canadians trained to counterattack. Then, in late 1941, when the Germans invaded Russia and the United States entered the war, aggressive action against Germany became a real prospect. A new emphasis on offensive tactics began in 1942; individual training was renewed and intensified.[15] Military exercises in the form of battle practice took place in Kent and on the Sussex Downs.

All This Training and Where Is the War?

> McNaughton wanted to fight, but he also worried — for
> good reason — that Canadian units and formations might be
> siphoned off piecemeal by British commanders. There was a
> strong possibility that colonial units and formations would be
> overused. This might well lead to heavy casualties.[16]

The latter part of 1939 and the first months of 1940 marked the so-called
Phoney War. On April 9, 1940, however, the period of calm ended when
the Germans marched into Norway and Denmark. On May 10, they
turned their attention to neutral Belgium and the Netherlands. Only
France remained to be subdued, after which Hitler would have control
of the coasts of Europe as far as the Pyrenees.

In April 1940, two battalions of the 2nd Canadian Infantry Brigade,
Princess Patricia's Canadian Light Infantry and The Edmonton Regiment,
a force of thirteen hundred troops considered the most advanced in
training, were organized for an attack on Trondheim, Norway. The
contingent left Aldershot for Scotland, where they awaited embarkation at
Dunfermline, but the embarkation and attack never took place.[17] Instead,
on April 20, the War Office cancelled the operation because of the risks
involved.[18] Orders were issued for the evacuation of British troops from
Norway. By early June, all Allied troops had withdrawn and Norway
remained in German hands until 1945.

On May 10, 1940, the tanks of Germany's panzer divisions rolled into
Belgium en route to smashing their way to the Channel. Hitler intended
for the British Expeditionary Force to be trapped in the Low Countries,
but the BEF had just enough time to escape to the French coast. Britain's
last toehold in France was in the north, on the Pas de Calais coast, but
the unstoppable German Army was closing in fast. British Headquarters
considered a last-ditch effort to hold on at Dunkirk. Commander-in-
Chief Lord John Gort, from his headquarters in France, called urgently

for reinforcements to relieve his increasingly perilous position. On May 24, 1940, Canadian units arrived at Dover— a dozen battalions and a field ambulance unit. There they waited until High Command decided there was no point in sending the Canadians across the Channel after all. The British were outnumbered, the French troops were in no mood to fight, the Belgian Army was weakening, and more troops would only add to the confusion. The Canadians returned to Aldershot but remained on alert until the evacuation of Dunkirk was complete.

As the Germans moved inexorably on Paris, the Chiefs of Combined Operations clung to the hope that a small part of coastal France could remain in Allied hands. Brittany seemed like a good choice as a centre of resistance, and the chiefs made plans to set up a redoubt there. On June 13, the 1st Brigade of the 1st Canadian Division received orders to proceed to France. Landed at Brest at dawn the next day, the troops marched through an unwelcoming town overflowing with refugees, and boarded a train bound for Le Mans, 322 kilometres inland. Here the 1st Brigade was to assemble in preparation for battle. Instead the news arrived that Paris had fallen, France had capitulated, and all resistance was at an end. Orders came for the troops to turn back for re-embarkation to England.

The trains carrying the Hastings and Prince Edward Regiment (Hasty Ps) and the Royal Canadian Regiment (RCR) halted forty-eight kilometres from Sablé near Le Mans to assemble, then returned to Brest. The two battalions boarded a waiting ship and sailed for Plymouth. A reluctant engineer took some persuasion to turn around the train carrying the 48th Highlanders, and when the troops arrived at a port, it turned out to be St-Malo. Just as well, as there was a British steamer in harbour with British troops already on board. Room was made for the Canadians and they reached Southampton that afternoon.[19] In the words of Transport Sergeant Basil Smith of the Hasty Ps, "But at least we saw a bit of France on our Cook's tour."[20]

By early June 1940, 338,000 British, French, and other Allied soldiers had escaped the German trap, but the wounded and all heavy equip-

London Canadian Memorial, Green Park. Inscription at the centre reads "In two world wars one million Canadians came to Britain and joined the fight for freedom. From danger shared, our friendship prospers." (Susan Evans Shaw)

ment had had to be abandoned.[21] Without the equipment, artillery, and ammunition, the British Expeditionary Force was essentially disarmed and of little use to defend the homeland until new armaments could be manufactured and distributed. The Canadians thus became vital to the task of defending England, and they prepared to give the Germans a shock should they land on British shores. To begin, the 1st Canadian Division moved to Northampton. McNaughton formed mobile columns using seven hundred vehicles of all types from Britain's stocks. The Germans might well invade the British coast before evacuated troops could be reorganized and rearmed, in which case there would not be enough equipped troops for defence. The only answer was to form a force that could be moved swiftly from place to place. The 1st Canadian Division was broken up into nine highly mobile columns renamed the Canadian Force, thus becoming Churchill's main reserve to be committed for major counteroffensive action. The field of operation stretched along the east coast from the River Thames in the south to the Humber in the north. Another of McNaughton's suggestions was to string wires "to trip the brutes" while keeping roads open for troop movements. Wires were strung over unoccupied aerodromes, flat spaces, and protected defiles in the South Downs country, some of which did succeed in bringing down German aircraft.[22]

Wilnis, Netherlands, Wilnis Memorial to three Canadian airmen and a Vickers Wellington Bomber HE 727. Returning from a raid over Dortmund, May 5, 1943, the plane was shot down by a German Messerschmitt 110 fighter plane. Two crew members parachuted out of the aircraft and were taken prisoner. The pilot managed to avoid the village, saving many lives, and crashed in a peat bog where the plane sank without a trace. Standing by the memorial is Jan Rouwenhorst, a history teacher who took part in the salvage and helped persuade the Government of Canada to participate. (Susan Evans Shaw)

In May 1940, Local Defence Volunteers (later called the Home Guard) had reported a serious shortage of rifles. McNaughton sent a request to Ottawa for thousands of World War I Ross rifles, reconditioned and stored since 1918, to be shipped to England. In the rain and mud of Flanders during the earlier war, Ross rifles had been a notorious liability, but in clean conditions among the civilian volunteers, the rifles proved a godsend.[23]

August 1940 marked the beginning of the Battle of Britain. The Luftwaffe attempted to wipe out the Royal Air Force, preparatory to a planned invasion of England. They had the numerical advantage, and had they concentrated on destroying RAF fighters, bombers, and radar, they might have won the battle and the war through sheer attrition. However, fate played into British hands when a fleet of German bombers overflew their target and by mistake bombed London's East End and Bethnal Green. In retaliation, Churchill ordered a string of bombing raids on German cities, including Berlin. Outraged, Reichsmarschall Hermann Göring made a fatal decision and switched targets from airfields to cities, in particular London.[24]

Graves in Wilnis General Cemetery of the three Canadian airmen whose bodies were found when the Vickers Wellington was unearthed in 2002. They were reburied with full military honours in the presence of members of the families of all five airmen. (Susan Evans Shaw)

Allied air groups, including Canadians, fought back in a battle that culminated in what could be designated the first Allied victory of the war. Ninety Canadian pilots flew with the RAF; twenty were killed in action. Although the German planes inflicted heavy bomb damage in vital areas of Britain, to say nothing of civilian lives destroyed, the Luftwaffe suffered serious losses of pilots and fighter planes, and never recovered strength.[25] The main onslaught of the Battle of Britain wound down at the end of October when the Luftwaffe switched to concentrate on night bombing of London and industrial sites elsewhere in the British Isles. The Blitz of London and other cities continued through the winter.[26]

By the beginning of 1941, when Britain in large part stood alone against the Nazis, Canada had sent ninety thousand airmen who would play a significant role in the bombing of Germany, although the first RCAF squadron was not commissioned until the middle of that year. The

1st Canadian Infantry Division was already in England. Two more divisions would arrive by early spring, followed by two armoured divisions,[27] and two Canadian battalions had been sent to garrison Hong Kong. The Canadian field force would spend forty-two months in Britain undergoing intensive training before being plunged into bloody campaigns in Italy in 1943 and Northwest Europe in 1944.[28]

Getting to Runnymede Air Forces Memorial, Surrey, England

The Air Forces Memorial at Runnymede commemorates by name more than 20,000 airmen, 3,034 of them Canadian, who were lost in the Second World War and have no known graves. They came from all parts of the Commonwealth and served in the Bomber, Fighter, Coastal, Transport, Flying Training, and Maintenance Commands. Also named are those airmen from occupied countries in Europe who served with the RAF. The memorial was designed by Sir Edward Maufe, with sculpture by Vernon Hill, and engraved glass and painted ceilings designed by John Hutton. Psalm 139:8-10 (also known as the "Airman's Psalm") is engraved on one of the gallery windows (page 33).[29]

If I climb up into Heaven, Thou art there;
If I go to Hell, Thou art there also.
If I take the wings of the morning
And remain in the uttermost parts of the sea,
Even there also shall Thy hand lead me;
And Thy right hand shall hold me.

By car: Take the M25 south from London to Junction 13. Take the A30 exit to London (W)/Hounslow/Staines, and at the roundabout take the second exit onto the A30/A308 ramp to Bagshot/Egham/Windsor. Merge onto The Glanty (A308) and continue to follow the A308 through one roundabout. At the next roundabout take the first exit onto Priest Hill (A328); follow A328 for 1.3 kilometres to Cooper's Hill Lane and turn left. Stay on Cooper's Hill Lane for about seven hundred metres; the Air Forces Memorial is on the left. There is parking at the entrance.

By public transit: Take the train from London Paddington Station toward Great Malvern and get off at the first stop, Slough. In Slough, walk to the town centre and bus station, bay 8. Take bus 71 to Englefield Green adjacent to Cooper's Hill Lane. From here it is an eleven-minute walk to the Air Forces Memorial.

Left: A bronze sculpture on the entrance doors to the Runnymede Air Forces Memorial. (Susan Evans Shaw)

Below: The Runnymede Air Forces Memorial, Surrey, England. The rooftop observation deck overlooks Runnymede Meadow where King John signed the Magna Carta. (Andrew Mathewson / Wikimedia Commons / CC BY-SA 2.0)

Runnymede Memorial, Surrey
Above: The "Airman's Psalm," Psalm
139:8-10, is engraved on the Great North
Window. (Susan Evans Shaw)

Left: Interior courtyard, Runnymede.
(Simon Davison / Flickr.com / CC BY 2.0)

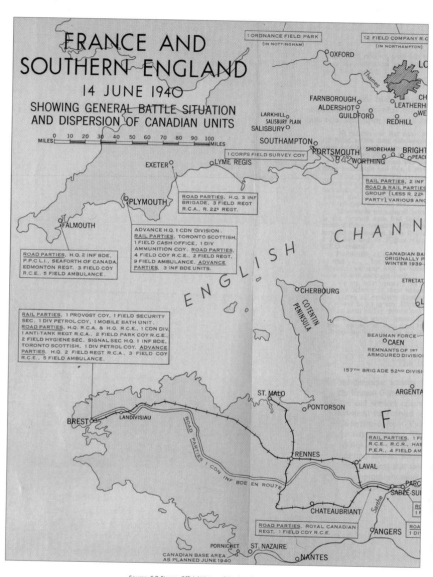

FRANCE AND SOUTHERN ENGLAND

14 JUNE 1940

SHOWING GENERAL BATTLE SITUATION
AND DISPERSION OF CANADIAN UNITS

MILES 0 10 20 30 40 50 60 70 80 90 100 MILES

1 ORDNANCE FIELD PARK (IN NOTTINGHAM)

12 FIELD COMPANY R.C.(IN NORTHAMPTON)

OXFORD

FARNBOROUGH
ALDERSHOT
GUILDFORD
REDHILL
LEATHERHEAD

LARKHILL
SALISBURY PLAIN
SALISBURY

SOUTHAMPTON
PORTSMOUTH
SHOREHAM
WORTHING
BRIGHTON
PEACE

1 CORPS FIELD SURVEY COY

EXETER
LYME REGIS

RAIL PARTIES, 2 INF
ROAD & RAIL PARTIES
GROUP (LESS R. 22e
PARTY), VARIOUS AND

PLYMOUTH

ROAD PARTIES, H.Q. 3 INF
BRIGADE, 3 FIELD REGT
R.C.A., R. 22e REGT.

FALMOUTH

ENGLISH CHANNE

ADVANCE H.Q. 1 CDN DIVISION,
RAIL PARTIES, TORONTO SCOTTISH,
1 FIELD CASH OFFICE, 1 DIV
AMMUNITION COY. ROAD PARTIES,
4 FIELD COY R.C.E., 2 FIELD REGT,
9 FIELD AMBULANCE. ADVANCE
PARTIES, 3 INF BDE UNITS.

ROAD PARTIES, H.Q. 2 INF BDE.,
P.P.C.L.I., SEAFORTH OF CANADA,
EDMONTON REGT. 3 FIELD COY
R.C.E., 5 FIELD AMBULANCE.

CANADIAN BAS
ORIGINALLY P
WINTER 1939-

CHERBOURG
COTENTIN
PENINSULA

ETRETAT

RAIL PARTIES, 1 PROVOST COY, 1 FIELD SECURITY
SEC., 1 DIV PETROL COY, 1 MOBILE BATH UNIT.
ROAD PARTIES, H.Q. R.C.A. & H.Q. R.C.E., 1 CDN DIV.
1 ANTI-TANK REGT R.C.A., 2 FIELD PARK COY R.C.E.,
2 FIELD HYGIENE SEC, SIGNAL SEC H.Q. 1 INF BDE,
TORONTO SCOTTISH, 1 DIV PETROL COY. ADVANCE
PARTIES. H.Q. 2 FIELD REGT R.C.A., 3 FIELD COY
R.C.E., 5 FIELD AMBULANCE.

BEAUMAN FORCE
CAEN
REMNANTS OF 1st
ARMOURED DIVISION

157TH BRIGADE 52ND DIVISI

ARGENTA

ST. MALO
PONTORSON

F

BREST
LANDIVISIAU

ROAD PARTIES 1 CDN INF BDE EN ROUTE

RENNES
LAVAL

RAIL PARTIES, 1 FI
R.C.E., R.C.R., HAS
P.E.R., 4 FIELD AM

PARC
SABLE SU
Sarthe

CHATEAUBRIANT

ROAD PARTIES, ROYAL CANADIAN
REGT, 1 FIELD COY R.C.E.

ANGERS

R
1 F

R
1 D

PORNICHET
ST. NAZAIRE

CANADIAN BASE AREA
AS PLANNED JUNE 1940

NANTES

Source: C.P. Stacey, *Official History of the Canadian Army in the Second World War. Volume I: Six Years of War: The Army in Canada, Britain and the Pacific* (Ottawa: Queen's Printer, 1966), map 7.

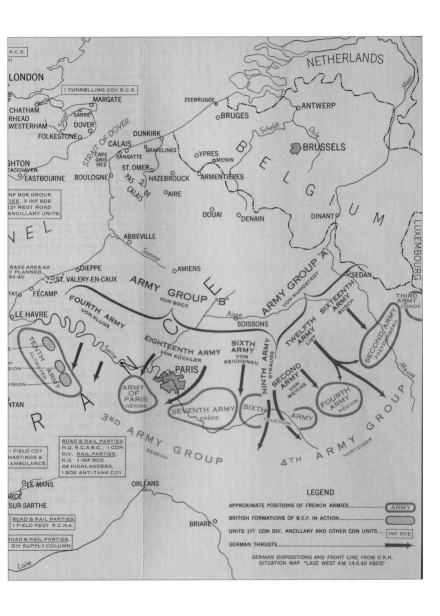

LONDON

1 TUNNELLING COY R.C.E.

CHATHAM
RHEAD
WESTERHAM
FOLKESTONE
MARGATE
SARRE
DOVER

STRAIT OF DOVER
CAPE GRIS NEZ

GHTON
EACEHAVEN
EASTBOURNE

DUNKIRK
CALAIS
GRAVELINES
SANGATTE
ST. OMER
HAZEBROUCK
BOULOGNE
AIRE

PAS DE CALAIS

ZEEBRUGGE
BRUGES
ANTWERP

NETHERLANDS

Maas

Scheldt

BRUSSELS

Dyle

B E L G I U M

YPRES
MENIN
ARMENTIÈRES

DOUAI
DENAIN

DINANT

LUXEMBOURG

INF BDE GROUP.
TIES, 3 INF BDE
2² REGT ROAD
ANCILLARY UNITS.

V E L

ABBEVILLE

Somme

AMIENS

BASE AREA AS
Y PLANNED
39-40

TAT
ST. VALERY-EN-CAUX
DIEPPE
FÉCAMP

ARMY GROUP "B"
VON BOCK

ARMY GROUP "A"
VON RUNDSTEDT

SEDAN

THIRD
ARMY
CONDE

LE HAVRE

FOURTH ARMY
VON KLUGE

E

Aisne

SOISSONS

TWELFTH
ARMY
LIST

SIXTEENTH
ARMY
BUSCH

SECOND ARMY
FRIEDRIKBERG

Meuse

TENTH
ARMY
ALTMAYER

ISION

IVISION

NTAN

Seine

EIGHTEENTH ARMY
VON KÜCHLER

PARIS

SIXTH
ARMY
VON
REICHENAU

NINTH
ARMY
STRAUSS

SECOND
ARMY
VON
WEICHS

FOURTH
ARMY
REQUIN

R

A

3RD ARMY GROUP

ARMY OF PARIS
HÉRING

SEVENTH ARMY
FRÈRE

SIXTH
ARMY
TOUCHON

4TH ARMY GROUP

HUNTZIGER

BESSON

1 FIELD COY
HASTINGS &
AMBULANCE.

ROAD & RAIL PARTIES.
H.Q. R.C.A.S.C., 1 CDN
DIV. RAIL PARTIES.
H.Q. 1 INF BDE,
48 HIGHLANDERS,
1 BDE ANTI-TANK COY.

LE MANS

ORLÉANS

RCE
SUR-SARTHE

ROAD & RAIL PARTIES.
1 FIELD REGT R.C.H.A.

BRIARE

ROAD & RAIL PARTIES.
DIV SUPPLY COLUMN

Loire

LEGEND

APPROXIMATE POSITIONS OF FRENCH ARMIES .... ARMY

BRITISH FORMATIONS OF B.E.F. IN ACTION ....

UNITS 1ST CDN DIV, ANCILLARY AND OTHER CDN UNITS. INF BDE

GERMAN THRUSTS

GERMAN DISPOSITIONS AND FRONT LINE FROM O.K.H.
SITUATION MAP "LAGE WEST AM 14.6.40 ABDS"

Top: Hong Kong, Sai Wan War Cemetery. (Gillian Chan)
Bottom: Hong Kong, Pinewood Battery. Remains of anti-aircraft gun emplacements. (Peter Dostal)

Hong Kong, Stanley Military Cemetary with Stanley Mound, now known as "The Twins." (Peter Dostal)

Left: Stanley Military Cemetery, "A la mémoire de nos Camarades" in foreground. Memorial to six French resistance fighters who took part in the defence of Hong Kong in December 1941, located on the site of a camp where prisoners were interned after the capitulation of the colony. (Peter Dostal)

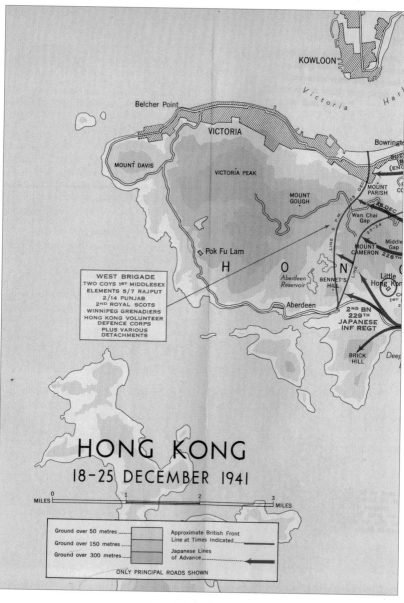

KOWLOON

Victoria Har

Belcher Point

VICTORIA

Bowringt

MOUNT DAVIS

VICTORIA PEAK

MOUNT PARISH

(ENG CO

MOUNT GOUGH

Wan Chai Gap

Middle Gap

MOUNT CAMERON 228TH

Pok Fu Lam

H O N N

Aberdeen Reservoir

BENNET'S HILL

Little Hong Kon

CO 1ST

WEST BRIGADE
TWO COYS 1ST MIDDLESEX
ELEMENTS 5/7 RAJPUT
2/14 PUNJAB
2ND ROYAL SCOTS
WINNIPEG GRENADIERS
HONG KONG VOLUNTEER
DEFENCE CORPS
PLUS VARIOUS
DETACHMENTS

Aberdeen

2ND BN
229TH
JAPANESE
INF REGT

BRICK HILL

Deep

HONG KONG
18–25 DECEMBER 1941

0   1   2   3
MILES   MILES

Ground over 50 metres	Approximate British Front Line at Times Indicated
Ground over 150 metres	
Ground over 300 metres	Japanese Lines of Advance

ONLY PRINCIPAL ROADS SHOWN

Source: C.P. Stacey, *Official History of the Canadian Army in the Second World War. Volume I: Six Years of War: The Army in Canada, Britain and the Pacific* (Ottawa: Queen's Printer, 1966), map 7.

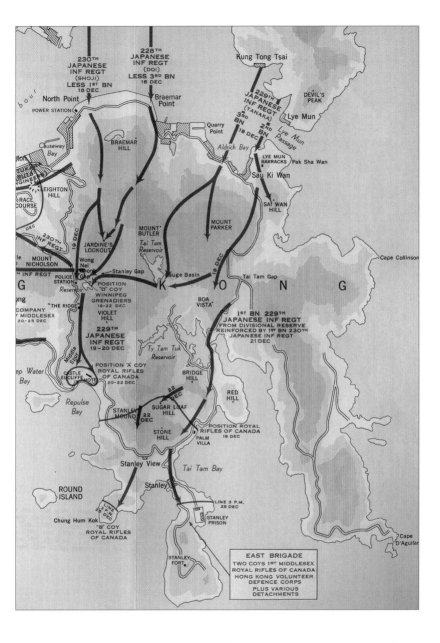

Hong Kong, The Central Cenotaph War Memorial. (Peter Dostal)

Part II
The Canadians in Hong Kong

That the Canadian volunteer soldier was excellent raw material of unmatched willingness can hardly be doubted. He simply manifested a burning desire to get into action. . . . Canadian soldiers in the Hong Kong garrison found themselves in the thick of an impossible struggle. They nonetheless held out with their imperial comrades for 17 days, proving that regardless of their state of training, Canadian troops were prepared to fight tenaciously and die hard.[1]

The British colony of Hong Kong embodied a choice morsel of European colonial wealth much coveted by Japan. Capture of the island and its territory signalled the opening gambit of Japan's master plan to rid southern Asia of European powers while at the same time expanding the reach of the Japanese Empire.

In the early 1930s preparations got under way. Espionage agents from Japan and Taiwan had long since infiltrated Hong Kong as shopkeepers and embassy personnel circulating among the ruling British and gentrified Chinese. Legions of these spies produced masses of data—so much so that, when the Japanese attacked Hong Kong in 1941, they were able to work with a scale map of defence installations that was complete and accurate in every detail.[2] British Prime Minister Winston Churchill had little interest in safeguarding Hong Kong. He saw no point in wasting reinforcements on the indefensible island. In his opinion there was "not the slightest chance of holding Hong Kong or of relieving it." As far as he was concerned the issue of Hong Kong could be settled by peace treaty after the war.[3]

But in 1941 the Chiefs of Staff in Britain had a change of heart. Underestimating Japanese strength and uncertain of the level of preparedness of Hong Kong territorial defences, they decided to strengthen the Hong Kong garrison. Rather than use British troops, they sent a telegram to Canada requesting one or two battalions. The Canadians had no intelligence organization of their own capable of assessing the situation in the Far East and no inkling of Churchill's opinion of Hong Kong's indefensibility. Prime Minister Mackenzie King in his capacity as Secretary of State for External Affairs promptly cabled back an agreement in principle to send two battalions and to arrange for their dispatch.[4]

The two Class "C" battalions selected for Hong Kong had no field experience and had not been among those recommended for operational consideration. In other words, they were intended for training in home defence back in Canada.

The Royal Rifles of Canada were an English-speaking battalion from Quebec City that included a substantial number of bilingual recruits. Mobilized July 8, 1940, the battalion had been sent to Newfoundland that winter. After their return to Quebec in August 1941 they were next assigned defence duty at Saint John, New Brunswick. Their commander was Lieutenant-Colonel William James Home. The Winnipeg Grenadiers had been mobilized September 1, 1939, as a machine-gun battalion. They had been dispatched to Jamaica in 1940 and converted to a rifle battalion. For the assignment to Hong Kong they were commanded by Lieutenant-Colonel John Louis Robert Sutcliffe.

On October 27, 1941, British transport *Awatea* and her escorting ship HMCS *Prince Robert* set sail from Vancouver carrying 96 officers and 1,877 other ranks, including two medical officers, two nursing sisters, two officers of the Dental Corps, three chaplains, and a detachment of the Canadian Postal Corps. The Royal Rifles were at full strength but the Winnipeg Grenadiers were five officers and fifty-two other ranks under strength. Before departure eighty Grenadiers and seventy-one

Above: Infantrymen of "C" Company, Royal Rifles of Canada, aboard H.M.C.S. *Prince Robert* en route to Hong Kong, 15 November 1941. Mascot Sergeant Gander is in the foreground. (© Government of Canada. Reproduced with the permission of Library and Archives Canada (2014). Source: Library and Archives Canada/Department of National Defence fonds/PA-166999)

Right: Newfoundland dog. Height at shoulder 71 cm. Weight about 54 kg. (June Porter)

Rifles had been struck off strength for medical reasons. Four hundred and forty new men were then recruited, many undertrained and several underage, and none had obtained a high standard of training. In any case, the best-trained troops were being saved for Europe. Additions to the Hong Kong detachment included brigade headquarters and a signal section. Overall commander of the Canadian contingent was Brigadier John Kelburne Lawson, a Permanent Force officer. Included among the 109 recruits on *Prince Robert* was Sergeant Gander, the Royal Rifles' mascot, a massive Newfoundland dog acquired by the battalion, where else but in Gander, Newfoundland.

Four battalions from Britain and two from India were already stationed in Hong Kong. With the arrival of the Canadians the whole defence force, including non-combatants, numbered fourteen thousand under the command of General Officer Commanding (GOC) Hong Kong, Major-General Christopher Michael Maltby, an Indian Army officer. General Maltby estimated the actual strength of the fighting force at eleven thousand of very mixed composition, many deficient in training.[5] The actual number of infantrymen was 5,422 and the remainder comprised Royal Artillery, the Royal Engineers Hong Kong Defence Corps, and the Royal Navy.[6] All were deficient in special weaponry and ammunition.

The Gin Drinkers Line, a system of fortifications seventeen kilometres long, formed a kind of Asian Maginot Line and was just as effective. Manned by insufficient troops with insufficient training, this first line of defence was clearly inadequate. Yet the arrival of the Canadians only served to reinforce the complacent confidence of Hong Kong residents that the territory could be successfully defended. Add to this the unshakeable belief that the Japanese did not fight night battles because they had

Hong Kong, Pinewood Battery, the highest of all the defence batteries. Remains of anti-aircraft gun emplacements. (Peter Dostal)

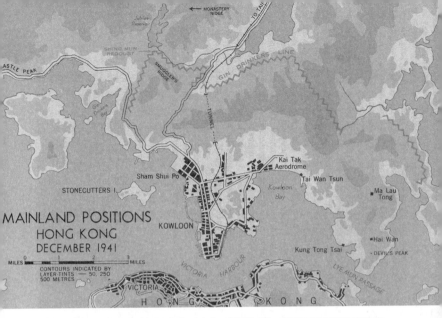

Source: C.P. Stacey, *Official History of the Canadian Army in the Second World War. Volume I: Six Years of War: The Army in Canada, Britain and the Pacific* (Ottawa: Queen's Printer, 1966), map 6.

exceptionally poor vision in the dark. Reassured in their misapprehension, the citizenry felt they had nothing to fear and the military found comfort in the certainty there would be no surprises. In anticipation of an attack from the sea, the southern part of the island was the heaviest fortified. With no navy, no air force, and no place to go, soldiers and civilians alike were sitting ducks in a trap.

The Battle

At 4:45 a.m. on December 8, 1941, the Japanese opened their assault by bombing the airport, and just after dawn bombs started to fall on Hong Kong proper. The alerted defenders manned every battle position ready for action, but without the heavy weaponry needed to counter air attacks, they were powerless. Moving swiftly and silently overland on rubber-soled shoes, the Japanese infantry reached the Gin Drinkers Line on December 10 and breached it with the ease of pushing over matchsticks. Five days after the initial Japanese attack, the British and Canadian defenders in Kowloon found themselves in retreat. Commandeering any vessel that could float, they withdrew across Victoria Harbour to Hong Kong Island.[7]

The rapid capture of the Kowloon Peninsula encouraged the Japanese infantry to follow up with an immediate attack on Hong Kong Island before the defenders could reorganize. Contrary to another mistaken belief that Japanese were no sailors on account of a tendency to seasickness, the Japanese easily crossed from the mainland to the island. There they landed at four points on the lightly defended north shore. With skill and energy the enemy attacked simultaneously at separated points. The brunt of the first attack across the Lye Mun Passage fell on the 5/7 Rajput Battalion manning the shore pillboxes. From their defence positions, the Rajputs took a considerable toll with machine guns and mortars before being overrun. Taking no prisoners, the Japanese moved quickly to their objective, the Sai Wan Fort on a hill overlooking the Lye Mun Barrack and defended by "C" Company of the Royal Rifles. Fifth columnists had already seized the fort. "C" Company counterattacked without taking the fort but nonetheless managed to inflict heavy losses on the attacking Japanese.

In the course of battle the Japanese lobbed grenades at the Canadians, who simply lobbed them back. But one grenade fell in front of seven wounded and helpless Rifles. Mascot Sergeant Gander "shot forward, grabbed the grenade in his mouth, and took off running." As the dog headed down the road toward the enemy, the grenade exploded.[8] Sergeant Gander gave his life and saved the seven soldiers. He was awarded a posthumous Dickin Medal, the animal equivalent of the Victoria Cross.

On the west half of the island, the defending Winnipeg Grenadiers captured a hill known as Mount Butler. "A" Company held a small depression within grenade-throwing distance of the enemy. As the enemy threw grenades at the Company, Sergeant-Major John Robert Osborn picked up each one and threw it back. One grenade landed out of reach. Shouting a warning, Osborn threw himself on the grenade, which exploded, killing him instantly and saving the lives of the rest of the Company. For his bravery, Osborn was awarded a posthumous Victoria Cross.

Before Brigadier Lawson could withdraw his headquarters on Wong Nei Chong Gap Road to a safer location, the Japanese surrounded his shelter. In his last radio communication, Lawson reported "They're all around us. I'm going outside to shoot it out." No one witnessed his death. Every member of his staff and of the Royal Scots ordered to reinforce the Gap died in the encounter.[9] The details of Lawson's death are unknown, but the Japanese buried him with military honours as they were wont to do for a soldier who died heroically.

Early on the morning of Christmas Day, an advanced guard of Japanese soldiers reached Fort Stanley. They entered an emergency hospital at St. Stephen's College and bayoneted fifty-six wounded soldiers, mostly Canadians, in their beds. The bayonets penetrated bodies and went right through the mattresses; the violence left gutters running with blood. The three nurses were raped and murdered. More atrocities occurred against the British patients and nurses at Victoria Hospital. But the worst savagery was shown to the non-Europeans — the Chinese and

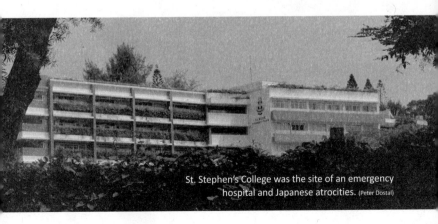

St. Stephen's College was the site of an emergency hospital and Japanese atrocities. (Peter Dostal)

the Indians were slaughtered wholesale. Later, after the surrender, the Japanese commander saw to the execution of those identified with the murder of the Canadians and British but the atrocities against the non-Europeans went unpunished.[10]

By the afternoon of Christmas Day 1941, General Maltby decided that more fighting meant more useless slaughter. A white flag was hoisted and Hong Kong fell to the Japanese.[11] Among the Canadians, a total of 23 officers and 267 other ranks were killed or died of wounds, including some murdered by the Japanese when trying to surrender. Of the British, Colonial, and Indian forces, there were approximately 955 all ranks killed or died of wounds and 659 missing.[12]

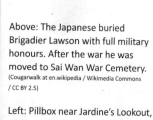

In seventeen days, from the opening salvos of the Battle of Hong Kong to the hoisting of the white flag, the outnumbered defenders inflicted substantially more than 3,000 casualties on the Japanese, including 675 killed. As well, the defenders succeeded against the invaders inasmuch as they delayed subsequent operations of the Japanese sweep through East and Southeast Asia. [13]

Above: The Japanese buried Brigadier Lawson with full military honours. After the war he was moved to Sai Wan War Cemetery. (Cougarwalk at en.wikipedia / Wikimedia Commons / CC BY 2.5)

Left: Pillbox near Jardine's Lookout, a hill overlooking Wong Nei Chong Gap. (Henry Chan)

Hong Kong, Stanley Military Cemetery, Cross of Sacrifice. (Peter Dostal)

Getting to the Cemeteries and Memorials[14]

Stanley Military Cemetery

There are 19 Canadians among the 427 identified burials, as well as a monument to the victims of the hospital massacre.

By car: From Exchange Square head north on Harbour View Street then make a slight left to merge onto Route 4 and continue for 2.5 kilometres to Route 1. Turn right toward Happy Valley/Aberdeen, a partial toll road, for four kilometres. Take exit 4 toward Shouson Hill/Stanley then merge onto Wong Chuk Hang Road and continue onto Island Road. After 2.1 kilometres you will arrive at a roundabout. Take the second exit onto Repulse Bay Road and continue onto Stanley Gap Road. At the roundabout take the second exit to Wong Ma Kok Road. Stanley Military Cemetery is seven hundred metres on the left.

By public transit: From Exchange Square take the no. 6 bus toward Stanley Prison and get off at Stanley Village Bus Terminus. The walk to Stanley Military Cemetery takes about fifteen minutes.

Stanley Military
Cemetery entrance.
(Peter Dostal)

The Hong Kong Memorial to the Chinese is inscribed with the names of 941 casualties of World War I and 1,493 casualties of World War II. The inscription in English and Chinese reads "in memory of the Chinese who died loyal to the Allied cause in the wars of 1914-18 and 1939-45." Stanley Military Cemetery. (Peter Dostal)

Sai Wan War Cemetery

Sai Wan Memorial forms the entrance to the War Cemetery and lists the names of 228 Canadians including J.R. Osborn, VC, among the more than 2,000 with no known grave. In all, there are 1,505 burials in the cemetery; 444 are unidentified and 175 are Canadian. Brigadier Lawson's grave is in section VIII, Row C, Grave 27.

By car: Follow eastbound Route 4 from Hong Kong Station for 12 kilometres. At the roundabout take the second exit onto Wan Tsui Road. After 290 metres turn left onto Lin Shing Road, then first right onto Cape Collinson Road. Sai Wan War Cemetery is on the right.

By public transit: Take the MTR (Mass Transit Railway) to Chai Wan and either take a taxi or a green minibus No. 16M toward Stanley.

On foot: From Chai Wan head north to Lok Man Road and turn left, then turn left again onto Chai Wan Road. At the roundabout take the second exit to Wan Tsui Road and then left onto Lin Shing Road. Take

Left: Sai Wan Memorial bears the names of more than two thousand Commonwealth servicemen who died in the Battle of Hong Kong or in captivity and who have no known grave. Sergeant-Major John Robert Osborn's name is among those inscribed. (Henry Chan)

Below left: Hong Kong, Sai Wan War Cemetery. (Gillian Chan)

the first right onto Cape Collinson Road. The distance is two kilometres and takes approximately half an hour.

Sai Wan Battery coordinates 22°16'21"N 114°14'6"S. From the Battery, the Japanese invasion landing place at Lei Yue Mun can be seen.

By car: From the Sai Wan War Cemetery head southwest along Cape Collinson Road to Shek O Road and turn right. At the roundabout take the second exit to Tai Tam Road and after 2.4 kilometres turn left onto Chai Wan Road, then after 550 metres turn right onto A Kung Ngam Road. Near the entrance to Lei Yue Mun Park, walk up to the summit of Sai Wan Hill.

By public transit: Take the MTR to Shai Kei Wan Station and a taxi to just before Lei Yue Mun Park, where a concrete path takes you to the summit of Sai Wan Hill.

The Gin Drinkers Line to the north of Kowloon Peninsula, a defensive string of trenches, pillboxes, and bunkers in the style of the German Siegfried Line and the French Maginot Line, extended from Gin Drinkers Bay in the west Via the Shing Mun Reservoir and Redoubt to Port Shelter on the eastern side of the New Territories. Undermanned by the defenders, the fall of the **Shing Mun Redoubt** left the Kowloon Peninsula open to the invading Japanese.

By public transit: Take the MTR to Tsuen Wan Station, then walk seven hundred metres to Shek Wai Kok Estate Shek Lin House and catch the no. 82 minibus toward Shing Mun Reservoir. From the Shing Mun Park Visitor Centre, walk 1.5 kilometres to the Shing Mun Redoubt. The tunnels of the Redoubt should be plainly visible on the left-hand side of the track.

Hong Kong, Entry of the galleries from Shing Mun Redoubt, part of the Gin Drinkers Line in. (Mike-tango, www.mablehome.com / Wikimedia Commons / CC BY-SA 3.0)

By car: Private cars can go directly to the Shing Mun Park Visitor Centre on weekdays only. From Tsuen Wan Ferry Pier head northeast on Tai Ho Road for 750 metres. Turn right onto Sha Tsui Road, then first left onto Tai Ho Road for 650 metres. At Tsuen Kam Interchange take the fifth exit to Wai Tsuen Road. Turn left onto Shek Wai Kok Road and continue onto Yi Pei Chun Road. At the roundabout take the second exit to Wo Yi Hop Road. Turn left onto Shing Mun Road and continue for 1 kilometre before turning left, then a sharp right to Shing Mun Park Visitor Centre. From there, it is a 1.5-kilometre walk to the Shing Mun Redoubt.

Wong Nai Chung Gap Road

This was the headquarters of Brigadier Lawson. Sites of interest are to be found nearby, but the grave marker at Brigadier Lawson's original burial place was demolished after the war.

By car: From Exchange Square head north on Harbour View Street, then make a slight left onto Route 4. Continue for about two kilometres to the exit on the right to Route 1 toward Happy Valley/Aberdeen. After

Hong Kong, before Brigadier Lawson could withdraw from his headquarters on Wong Nei Chong Gap Road to a safer location, the Japanese surrounded his shelter. (Henry Chan)

eight hundred metres take the exit toward Happy Valley and merge onto Wong Nai Chung Road. Turn right onto Queen's Road East then left onto Stubbs Road for two kilometres. Continue to Wong Nai Chung Gap Road.

By public transit: Take the no. 6 bus toward Stanley Prison to the Wong Nai Chung Reservoir Park and Wong Nai Chong Gap Road.

Ottawa, Ontario, The Hong Kong Veterans Memorial Wall

Located near Sussex Drive in Ottawa, this wall is inscribed with the names of the Canadians who fought to defend Hong Kong. On one side are the names of the 961 members of The Royal Rifles; on the other are the names of the 911 Winnipeg Grenadiers. On either end are listed the 106 members of brigade headquarters, including doctors, dentists, nurses, and chaplains. A cross indicates those who died. At the insistence of Hong Kong veterans, Sergeant Gander is listed with the Royal Rifles of Canada.
(Susan Evans Shaw)

Dover Castle, landward aspect.

(Susan Evans Shaw)

The port of St-Malo, France.

Part III

Crossing from England to Northwest Europe

In the sea-port of Saint Malo 'twas a smiling morn in May
When the Commodore Jacques Cartier to the westward sailed
  away;
In the crowded old Cathedral all the town were on their knees
For the safe return of kinsmen from the undiscover'd seas;
And every autumn blast that swept o'er pinnacle and pier
Filled manly hearts with sorrow and gentle hearts with fear.[1]

The west coast of France holds great significance for Canadians. From St-Malo, as celebrated in the verses by Thomas D'Arcy McGee, Jacques Cartier, a Breton explorer, set sail for the New World and claimed Canada for France. Samuel de Champlain, founder of Quebec and explorer of eastern Canada, was born at Brouage,[2] fifty kilometres south of La Rochelle on the Bay of Biscay. Many of his voyages began at Honfleur, across the Seine estuary from Le Havre.[3]

Today there are at least ten different ferry routes across the English Channel. The fastest and least expensive is the Dover-Calais route; ferries run thirty-three times daily and make the crossing in an hour and a half. Other ferry options to France include Newhaven-Dieppe, twice daily, duration four hours; Portsmouth-Caen, three times daily, duration five hours, forty-five minutes; Portsmouth-Cherbourg, twelve times weekly, duration three hours; and Portsmouth-Le Havre, seven times weekly, duration six hours. There are also ferries to Belgium and Holland.

If you choose to cross by the Channel Tunnel (Chunnel), you and your car are loaded onto a specially designed train boxcar for the thirty-five-minute crossing. If you prefer to travel by rail, the Eurostar high-speed

Town of Dover, England, and harbour from Dover Castle keep. (Susan Evans Shaw)

train leaves London's St. Pancras Station and makes one stop at Ashford International before a swift trip through the Chunnel to Calais.

While you are in Dover I recommend taking an extra day to visit Dover Castle. Those wanting a good workout can climb the steps from Castle Road to the pay booth outside the castle walls. For the less energetic, a winding road ascends the cliff, and there is free parking with space for two hundred vehicles. City buses also make the climb to the castle entrance. A tour through Dover Castle is a tour through

Dover Castle. Roman Pharos and Saxon church with Henry II's castle keep, background left.
(Susan Evans Shaw)

Dover Castle. Balcony from wartime tunnels overlooking the harbour. (Susan Evans Shaw)

Right: Entrance to wartime tunnels, Dover Castle. Photography is forbidden in the underground facility and hospital. (Susan Evans Shaw)

VICE ADMIRAL DOVER

FIXED DEFENCES DOVER

English history. Because of its strategic location on the coast closest to France, the site has been occupied since earliest times. A sturdy stone lighthouse (Pharos) built by the Romans stands at the highest point next to a Saxon church that is still used for services and for years was a chapel for the military stationed at the barracks. Farthest away from the cliff's edge and half-submerged in the ground are the ruins of a medieval fortress. In the centre of the promontory, dominating the skyline, is the castle keep built by Henry II.

Of most relevance to World War II sites are the secret wartime tunnels under the castle, which have been in use for military purposes since the Napoleonic Wars. Now restored and open for tours, the warren of rooms includes the war room with its great round table covered in maps and bristling with telephones and other communication devices of the period. Planning for the evacuation of Dunkirk took place here. A separate tour features the underground hospital with its facilities.

There is a small museum next to the cafeteria located in one of several eighteenth-century barracks. Just inside the entrance stands a remarkable seven-metre large bore cannon known as Queen Elizabeth's Pocket Pistol. Cast in Utrecht in 1544, a striking feature of the cannon is the wealth of Renaissance ornament, including panels in relief of allegorical figures such as Victory and Liberty.[4]

Nearby can be seen a circular object, about one metre in diameter, somewhat resembling a very large yo-yo. Rusty but mostly intact, this is a prototype bouncing bomb recovered in 1996 off Reculver beach near Canterbury, Kent. The bombs were designed for use by the RAF dam busters in their attempt to flood the Ruhr Valley. The attack took place on May 16, 1943. Dropped by low-flying Lancasters, the bombs bounced along the surface of the water until, on collision with the concrete surface of the dam, they exploded. The attack succeeded to a limited extent—two of the three targeted dams were breached, flooding the area, destroying or damaging factories and, even more devastating, knocking out hydro-electric power in the area. Of the 113 airmen who took off for the raid, thirty were Canadian, fourteen of whom were killed in the raid and one taken prisoner.

Dover Castle museum. Prototype bouncing bomb recovered in 1996 off Reculver beach near Canterbury, Kent. (Susan Evans Shaw)

The Raid on Dieppe, August 19, 1942

> So far as any one individual had general authority over the operation, it was the Chief of Combined Operations, Lord Louis Mountbatten; but obviously his powers were circumscribed. The fact is that the Dieppe plan was the work of a large and somewhat indefinitely composed committee, whose composition, moreover, changed steadily as the planning proceeded. . . . There were a great many cooks, and this probably had much to do with spoiling the broth.[5]

The Strategy

Two and a half years after the beginning of hostilities, the war in the west was being fought in the air and on the seas, but other than in North Africa, nothing much was happening on land. Apart from a couple of successful but extremely costly raids at St-Nazaire and Bruneval, there was no sign of plans for an assault on Germany's dominance over Europe. Moreover, Churchill was under pressure from Stalin to open a second front and distract the German Army from its attack on Russia. President Roosevelt and the American public wanted to see some action by American troops now stationed in England. Canadian General Andy McNaughton was eager to see his thoroughly trained Canadian troops in action. And, most of all, the British public, which had stoically withstood the nightmare of the Blitz, longed for some sign of aggression against the Germans.

For all these reasons, Combined Operations Headquarters felt itself under considerable pressure to plan a major raid on the coast of France. In the course of an administrative shuffle at the end of October 1941, Prime Minister Winston Churchill appointed Lord Louis Mountbatten to the post of Chief of Combined Ops. Mountbatten's youth (he was only forty) and vigour (he was noted for working hard and playing hard) made him seem the ideal choice as aging veterans of World War I were gradually being retired from command. The prime minister's appointment of such

Dieppe, Blue Beach, Water-smoothed gravel impeded tanks and slowed soldiers on foot. (Anthony G. Nutkins)

a man to the important job of organizing combined assaults encouraged the public to hope that at last they were going to see some action against the Germans who were occupying France.

Dieppe made the best sense as an objective because of its proximity to the harbour and aerodrome at Newhaven on the Sussex coast. The distance, 108 kilometres, would allow fighter aircraft to fly over and back without running short of fuel while preliminary bombing was carried out. British intelligence, moreover, reported that Dieppe was not heavily defended. Better still, the beaches appeared eminently suitable for landing infantry and armoured fighting vehicles.

The outline plan for the raid was exceedingly ambitious. A force of infantry, airborne troops, and armoured fighting vehicles would capture Dieppe and hold the town. There would be a heavy bomber attack of the dock area. Meanwhile, troops would destroy enemy defences in the town and the aerodrome installation at St-Aubin. Radar stations, power stations, rail facilities, and petrol dumps would all be destroyed. The operation complete, the troops would re-embark for home, and all this was to be done in the space of one tide, a period of roughly six hours.

Clementine Churchill, however, who had passed summer holidays in Dieppe before the war, warned her husband that the cliff walls were honeycombed with caves, ideal for concealing guns.[6] As well, no one told the planners about the slippery stone and shale beaches, which would make the operation of tanks, with their caterpillar tracks, next to impossible. Nor did anyone consider how difficult such a surface would be underfoot.

Why the Canadians?

[Lieutenant-General Harry] Crerar had been growing very weary of Canada's war bureaucracy. He was beginning to feel that the war was passing him by. So far, his war had been all tea cups and paperclips.[7]

By 1941, Canadians had tired of Prime Minister Mackenzie King's all-talk, no-action approach to the war. They were calling for blood. From every quarter of the country could be heard criticism of the army's continued inactivity. The prime minister's response finally came in August 1941. To save his political hide, Mackenzie King sent word to Whitehall that Canadian volunteers could serve in any theatre of war. To General McNaughton's great relief, he at last received from Cabinet the authority to undertake raids and operations without having to ask for permission in each case.[8] Having been given carte blanche, McNaughton left in January 1942 on three months' medical leave to Canada, and Lieutenant-

General Harry Crerar took over as acting Corps commander. Eager to see battle, Crerar lobbied the British hard to get his Canadian troops some action. That same year, the Canadian troops in England came under the operational command of Lieutenant-General Bernard Montgomery. Training policy for the Canadian Army now shifted from a defensive role to offensive action in preparation for the ultimate Allied goal of an invasion. All ranks learned to assess a battle situation, issue brief orders in the event that officers were incapacitated, then swing immediately into attack, each step done at top speed. This training, drilled repeatedly, put the men in top physical and mental condition.

Operation Sledgehammer

> The raid on Dieppe was parented by duplicity from within and pressure from without.[9]

The plan for the raid on Dieppe originated in April 1942 at Combined Operations Headquarters. Churchill undertook a commitment to the Americans to stage a mini-invasion by British troops on the French coast, in an operation called Sledgehammer. No one dared mention that the British did not have the capability to implement such a promise. Churchill, however, under American pressure, simply quailed at the prospect of telling Roosevelt the operation was impossible. Better to provide an alternative that would distract attention from Sledgehammer. So the idea for a large-scale raid on Dieppe was born.

Mountbatten's original plan had been a small operation involving five hundred Marines and commandos in a hit-and-run operation, targeting an important German radar installation at Dieppe as follow-up to the successful Bruneval raid in February. To cover up for the foot-dragging over the implementation of Sledgehammer, Combined Ops Headquarters scrapped Mountbatten's original plan, and, in response to Crerar's lobbying and in the face of plain common sense, gave the job to

Canadian troops embarking in landing craft during a training exercise before the raid on Dieppe, France, c. 1942.
(Library and Archives Canada, PA-113244)

the 2nd Canadian Division. The courage and zeal of the Canadians was never in question, but they had no experience of an amphibious or any other operation.[10] The planners chose to be blinkered to the fact that Dieppe was better suited as a target for a raid of five hundred men rather than the five thousand who were eventually sent. In the opinion of Colonel Brian McCool of the Royal Regiment of Canada, by expanding the operation, the raid on Dieppe lost three winning factors: mobility, surprise, and experienced assaulters.

Operation Rutter

Combined Ops initially planned the raid for early July. In preparation, Canadian troops arrived at the Isle of Wight to practise invasion tactics on terrain very similar to what they would find at Dieppe. "Her lush, rolling meadows, broad beaches and sheer cliffs offered the troops near-perfect training facilities for combined assault."[11] But for the Canadians this was just another training exercise, only much tougher than ones they had previously undergone.

On July 2, 1942, the Canadian troops marched onto infantry landing ships moored on the Solent, the strait between the Isle of Wight and the Hampshire coast. General Montgomery ordered that other ranks not be told where they were headed or for what purpose. Only after the men

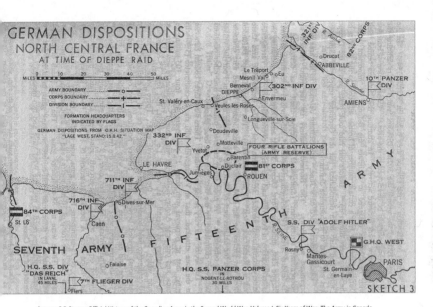

GERMAN DISPOSITIONS
NORTH CENTRAL FRANCE
AT TIME OF DIEPPE RAID

Source: C.P. Stacey, *Official History of the Canadian Army in the Second World War. Volume I: Six Years of War: The Army in Canada, Britain and the Pacific* (Ottawa: Queen's Printer, 1966), 353, sketch 3.

were sealed aboard did officers inform them that this was in fact a real operation and plans were to sail that night for Dieppe.

Events did not go according to plan. In the night, the weather abruptly became unfavourable, and the crossing was postponed for twenty-four hours. Five days later, with no improvement in the weather, thousands of men remained crammed into space intended only for overnight, and with supplies dwindling, Churchill and Montgomery reluctantly realized a decision had to be made. Then, a Luftwaffe pilot on routine reconnaissance spotted the concentration of shipping in the Solent. An opportunity too good to pass up, four German planes swooped down, aiming machine guns and cannon on the flotilla. They succeeded only in damaging two troopships and slightly injuring four men sleeping on deck, but their action forced the commanders' hand. The following day

Montgomery cancelled the operation. Disappointed troops disembarked and dispersed to Aldershot.

Meanwhile, anticipating an invasion of the French coast but without specific knowledge of an impending attack, the Germans strengthened vulnerable defences. At the beginning of August 1942, Hitler ordered construction of an impregnable "Atlantic Wall," a fortification that would run without a break along the Atlantic and Channel coasts. From maps and air reconnaissance, British intelligence knew of the wall and pillboxes on the main Dieppe beach, but nothing of the massed armaments, beach defences, and anti-tank guns or the location of regimental command posts. In sum, the situation for a landing on the French coast would be hazardous at best. By the time of the August raid, a supremely well-fortified Dieppe garrisoned by a greatly strengthened German Army waited in a state of full alert.[12]

Operation Jubilee

> This raid came of very much surprise to me as the security this time was excellent as far as we are concerned because we never knew a thing about it till we were on the mother ship in one of the ports of England and at the present time I am very excited but very eager to go although I am somewhat serious [?curious] but tomorrow night our fate shall be decited [sic] and I have a feeling it will be a good fate. Now as we are on the Road to Dieppe I will close now. Your ever loving son, George xxxx[13]

Throughout the period of false starts and mishaps, the public in Allied countries continued to call for action. Meanwhile, ever greater German advances in Russia made diversionary aid essential. After three years of one German triumph after another, something needed to be done if only to boost morale of the public, of the military, and of the powers at Combined Operations Headquarters.

Plans for a second try at a raid got under way. Montgomery, who had left to take over Allied forces in North Africa, delegated General Crerar with military responsibility for a new operation, codenamed Jubilee. The naval force constituted 237 ships and landing craft, and sixteen minesweepers. The landing force would consist of 6,100 all ranks, of whom 4,963 were Canadian and 1,075 British, along with 50 American observers and 5 anti-Nazi enemy nationals. A Canadian, Major-General Hamilton Roberts, was placed in charge of the operation.[14] Owing to normal attrition, as many as 10 percent of the soldiers were fresh replacements. None had had the chance to undertake preliminary training at the Isle of Wight. They would have no choice but to learn on their feet.

The raid would involve attacks at five different points on a front of approximately sixteen kilometres, from right to left: Varengeville (Orange Beach), by British No. 4 Commandos; Pourville (Green Beach), by the South Saskatchewan Regiment and the Cameron Highlanders of Canada; Puys (Blue Beach), by the Royal Regiment of Canada; and Berneval (Yellow Beach), by British No. 3 Commandos. The main attack would go in on the long beach fronting Dieppe (White Beach on the right, Red Beach on the left), carried out by the Royal Hamilton Light Infantry (the Rileys), the Essex Scottish, Les Fusiliers Mont-Royal, the Royal Marine "A" Commando, and 14th Canadian Army Tank Regiment (Calgary Regiment).

To make the raid more difficult to detect beforehand, the force was not concentrated; instead, it embarked from five different ports on the evening

The Sea Wall at Puys, looking east.
(Source: C.P. Stacey, *Official History of the Canadian Army in the Second World War. Volume I: Six Years of War: The Army in Canada, Britain and the Pacific* (Ottawa: Queen's Printer, 1955), 370a)

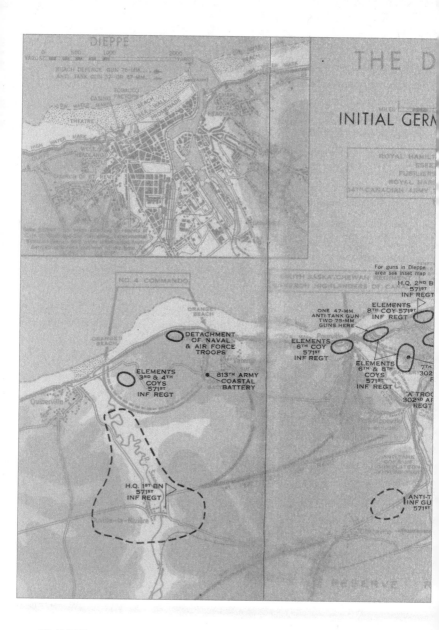

DIEPPE

BEACH DEFENCE GUN 75-MM.
ANTI-TANK GUN 37-OR 47-MM.

TOBACCO FACTORY

BEACH SEA WALL PROMENADE

THEATRE

CASINO HALL

WEST HEADLAND

CHURCH OF ST REMY

THE D

INITIAL GER

ROYAL HAMILT
ESSE
FUSILIERS
ROYAL MARI
14TH CANADIAN ARMY

For guns in Dieppe
area see inset map

NO. 4 COMMANDO

ORANGE
BEACH

SOUTH SASKATCHEWAN
ROYAL HIGHLANDERS OF CA

H.Q. 2ND B
571ST
INF REGT

ELEMENTS
8TH COY 571ST
INF REGT

ORANGE
BEACH

DETACHMENT
OF NAVAL
& AIR FORCE
TROOPS

ONE 47-MM.
ANTI-TANK GUN
TWO 75-MM.
GUNS HERE

ELEMENTS
6TH COY
571ST
INF REGT

Quiberville

ELEMENTS
3RD & 4TH
COYS
571ST
INF REGT

813TH ARMY
COASTAL
BATTERY

ELEMENTS
6TH & 8TH
COYS
571ST
INF REGT

7TH
302ND
R

"A" TROO
302ND AF
REGT

ANTI-TANK
GUN AND
INSTALLATION

H.Q. 1ST BN
571ST
INF REGT

ANTI-T
INF GU
571ST

Ville-la-Rivière

RESERVE
R

IEPPE OPERATION
19 AUGUST 1942

MAN DISPOSITIONS, DIEPPE AREA
19 AUGUST 1942

ON LIGHT INFANTRY
SCOTTISH
MONT-ROYAL
THE "A" COMMANDO
TANK REGT (CALGARY REGT)

ROYAL REGIMENT
OF CANADA

FIELD PICKET
1ST BN 570TH
INF REGT

2ND TROOP 770TH
ARMY COASTAL
BATTERY

H.Q. 3RD BN
571ST INF REGT

H.Q. 571ST
INF REGT

9TH COY
571ST
INF REGT

"B" TROOP
302ND ARTY
REGT

10TH COY
571ST
INF REGT

7TH COY
571ST
INF REGT
& NAVAL
COY

11TH COY
571ST
INF REGT

B TROOP
302ND ARTY
REGT

5TH COY
571ST
INF REGT

ELEMENTS
12TH COY 571ST
INF REGT

TROOP
ND ARTY
REGT

2ND COY 302ND
ENGINEER BN

1ST COY 302ND
ENGINEER BN

Map: Tracing layer indicating
initial German disposition, Dieppe
Operation, August 19, 1942.
(Source: C.P. Stacey, *Official History of the Canadian Army
in the Second World War. Volume I: Six Years of War:
The Army in Canada, Britain and the Pacific* (Ottawa:
Queen's Printer, 1955), map 5)

Below left: Dieppe (present
day), the main beach where the
Canadian 2nd Division landed on
August 19, 1942. (Anthony G. Nutkins)

Below right: The main beaches
at Dieppe. (Source: C.P. Stacey, *Official History of
the Canadian Army in the Second World War. Volume I:
Six Years of War: The Army in Canada, Britain and the
Pacific* (Ottawa: Queen's Printer, 1955), 370c)

of August 18. Bad luck struck in the pre-dawn hours, however, when ships of the eastern sector carrying No. 3 Commandos heading for Berneval collided with a German convoy sailing from Boulogne to Dieppe. A small sea battle ensued and gunfire alerted the defenders on the French coast. British escort vessels were seriously damaged and the landing craft scattered so that only seven succeeded in landing their troops. German defenders outnumbered the force put ashore, effectively blocking their attempt to reach the objective battery. Overwhelmed, 82 of 120 landed No. 3 Commandos were taken prisoner.

At the Varengeville Battery on the far right, No. 4 Commandos captured all their objectives exactly according to plan. They cleared battery positions and demolished the garrison, wholly eliminating a menace to shipping off Dieppe. For his gallant part in the action, Captain P.A. Porteous was awarded the Victoria Cross.[15]

On the left, at Puys, just west of Berneval, the Royal Regiment ran into trouble. Landing troops at a precise time and place in the dark required skill and luck, and success depended on surprise and darkness. Unfortunately, luck was not on the side of the Royals. The first wave of troops struck Blue Beach seventeen minutes late, and the remainder did not arrive for nearly another hour, losing the effects of darkness and of a smoke screen laid down by escort ships. Defenders on the beach had only to wait to open with machine-gun fire as landing craft lowered their ramps. Barbed wire, undetected by reconnaissance, topped the seawall, trapping the men on the beach. A machine-gun bunker disguised as a summer house had complete command of the beach. Murderous machine-gun fire made attempts to evacuate the Royals futile. Surviving remnants of the regiment surrendered. Grimmest of the whole grim operation, of 554 troops landed at Puys, 227 died on the beach.

In the Pourville area, sixty- to ninety-metre cliffs dominated Green Beach on both sides. Landing craft carrying the South Saskatchewan Regiment touched down without a hitch, achieving a measure of surprise,

Brookwood, Surrey, England This memorial honours 3,500 men and woman of Commonwealth land forces who gave their lives in World War II and have no known grave, among them, 200 Canadians. (Susan Evans Shaw)

Sicily, Catania War Cemetery, with Mount Etna in the distance.
(Commonwealth War Graves Commission)

Caserta War Cemetery, Italy. Burials include those who died in the hospitals as well as prisoners from a nearby prisoner-of-war camp.
(Commonwealth War Graves Commission)

Source: G.W.L. Nicholson, *Official History of the Canadian Army in the Second World War. Volume II: The Canadians in Italy, 1943-1945* (Ottawa: Queen's Printer, 1966), front endpaper.

SOUTHERN ITALY
10 JULY 1943 — 9 JUNE 1944

MILES 0   50   100 MILES

Terni
Rieti
GRAN SASSO MOUNTAINS
Pescara
Chieti
Francavilla
Orsogna
Ortona
Lanciano
ABRUZZI
LATIUM
ME
Arsoli
Collarmele
Avezzano
Sulmona
Popoli
Tivoli
Subiaco
MOLISE
Vasto
San Salvo
Petacciato
Termoli
Valmontone
Sora
Castel
Larino
Velletri
Frosinone
Caroville
Campobasso
San Severo
Anzio
Littoria
Fondi
Acquafondata
Venafro
Mignano
Raviscanina
Piedimonte d'Alife
Lucera
Foggia
ADRIATIC SEA
Terracina
Dragone
Alvignano
Benevento
Castelfranco
Barletta
Andria
San Spirito
Bari
PONTINE ISLANDS
Gulf of Gaeta
Gaeta
Capua
Volturno
Caserta
APULIA
Afragola
Avellino
Melfi
Altamura
Brindisi
Naples
Nocera
Baronissi
Salerno
CAMPANIA
Potenza
Taranto
Gulf of Naples
Sorrento
Gulf of Salerno
Ogliastro
LUCANIA
Gulf of Taranto
TYRRHENIAN SEA
Castrovillari
IONIAN
SEA
Crotone
CALABRIA
Catanzaro
Gulf of Sant'Eufemia
Gulf of Squillace
Gulf of Gioia
Palmi
Locri
Palermo
Messina
Villa San Giovanni
Trapani
Reggio Calabria
STR. OF MESSINA
SICILY
MOUNT ETNA
Adrano
Enna
Catania
Caltagirone
Augusta
Syracuse
Ragusa
SEA

Sicily, Agira Canadian War Cemetery looking toward Lago Pozzillo. (Commonwealth War Graves Commission)

Rome, Graves in the Rome War Cemetery below the
ancient Aurelian city wall. (Commonwealth War Graves Commission)

Below: Italy, Ancona War Cemetery. Inlaid marble walk from the entrance to the Cross of Sacrifice. (Commonwealth War Graves Commission)

Top: Cassino War Cemetery below Monte Cassino. (Commonwealth War Graves Commission)

Bottom: Reflecting pool surrounded by its border of inlaid marble. To the right and left are the stele of the Cassino Memorial listing the names of more than 4,000 soldiers with no known grave. (Commonwealth War Graves Commission)

but in the semi-darkness missed the objective astride the River Scie and landed to the west. The companies assigned the task of seizing the high ground had to penetrate the village in order to cross by a bridge, losing by this delay the advantage of the surprise landing.

Those operating west of Pourville occupied all their objectives, but those to the east had no such success. The trench system around Quatre Vents Farm adjacent to the radar station could not be taken.[16] The South Saskatchewans' commanding officer, Lieutenant-Colonel Cecil Merritt, by courageous example, got some 159 men over the bridge and into Pourville under steady machine-gun fire. As soon as his troops were across the bridge, Merritt located and, with a well-aimed grenade, destroyed the pillbox from which a German soldier was firing on the company.

The South Saskatchewans closed on the radar station only to find it too well defended, leaving no choice but to withdraw. In the chaos of the fighting, Sergeant Jack Nissenthall, a Royal Air Force officer serving temporarily with the South Saskatchewans, managed to crawl behind the radar station. Under heavy fire he cut the telephone lines, forcing the operators inside to use their radio, signals from which could be intercepted and decoded. London headquarters suddenly began receiving radio signals from Dieppe and could follow happenings on the beaches.[17]

The Cameron Highlanders of Canada landed astride the River Scie according to plan. As the troops disembarked, Sergeant Alex Graham piped them ashore to the tune "A Hundred Pipers." Unfortunately they arrived half an hour late, and their position caused the three companies to become separated. Their objective was to capture the aerodrome at St-Aubin in conjunction with the Calgary Tanks, but because the South Saskatchewans had not been able to clear Pourville and the headlands, and because the tanks remained pinned on the beach, the Camerons never achieved their objective. Nevertheless, their acting commander, Major Andrew Law, led a band of his men about two kilometres inland, the farthest penetration by any force that day.[18] Amid heavy losses and

Dieppe's pebble beach and cliff immediately following the raid on August 19th, 1942. A scout car has been abandoned
(Library and Archives Canada, C-029861)

unrelenting bombardment, the remainder of two companies of Camerons managed to reach landing craft on the beach.

Meanwhile, the frontal attack on Dieppe was to be delivered by the Royal Hamilton Light Infantry on the right and the Essex Scottish on the left. The landing craft made their approach without incident, and the infantry, backed by direct naval bombardment, touched down on the beach. The RAF laid down a smokescreen, and Hurricane fighters made a cannon attack on beach defences but completely missed their target. Tanks, late in disembarking, could give no support after naval and air support ceased. As a result, the enemy recovered quickly, and their return fire pinned down the Canadians. The impetus of the attack ebbed and the battle for Dieppe on the main beaches foundered. One group of Rileys broke into the casino, where they rounded up snipers, but then found themselves sheltering on the floor of a shack that turned out to have been used as a latrine.[19]

A total of twenty-nine tanks came off the landing craft. Two sank in deep water. Of the remaining twenty-seven that made it to shore, fifteen crossed the seawall only to be stopped by impenetrable concrete roadblocks. Unable to progress, they returned to the beach. Most of the tanks were immobilized by damage or bogged down in the steeply graded beach's pebbles. There, they acted as pillboxes, their armour giving protection from German anti-tank guns, but almost none of their crews returned to England, the men either killed or taken prisoner.

To add to the confusion, communications had broken down with Division HQ onboard the destroyer *Calpe*. There, the Commanding Officer, Hamilton Roberts, received only garbled messages and fragments of information, some of which may have come from German radio operators who had broken into the British system. Confused by conflicting reports, Roberts lost control of the battle. He sent in his last reserves, Les Fusiliers Mont-Royal, under the impression that the forces had succeeded in penetrating the town, but they were met with devastating fire that killed 119 as they landed. Attempts at rescue failed, and the survivors were captured.

As the enemy moved in, Brigadier William Southam of the 6th Infantry Brigade advised Lance-Corporal Lecky to burn his papers before attempting to get away. But the brigadier failed to burn his own papers, and when both men were taken prisoner, the Germans got their hands on Southam's operation orders. Among them was this instruction: "Wherever possible, prisoners' hands will be tied to prevent destruction of their documents." Because of this order and in the aftermath of a minor British raid on the Channel Island of Sark on October 4, from October 8, 1942, Canadians prisoners captured at Dieppe were shackled, and remained so until November 23 of the following year. [20]

As the raid collapsed, troops had to wade or swim through intense German fire to get to rescue craft. Few of them could swim, and snipers picked off floundering men like ducks in a bathtub. Already twice wounded, Lieutenant-Colonel Merritt, along with Major Claude Orme, also of the South Saskatchewans, set up a makeshift rearguard defence in a small bandstand on the shore. From its shelter they gave covering fire with machine guns and grenades until evacuation was complete. Although he could swim, Merritt refused to leave. He, Major Orme, and Padre Foote of the Rileys—who, under fire, continued to minister to the wounded—chose to stay with their boys. Merritt and Foote were awarded the Victoria Cross;[21] Orme was awarded the Distinguished Service Order.

Germans prodded the bushes to find Major Andrew Law and his small band of Camerons. Corporal Alec Graham laid down his sten gun and rifle — and his bagpipes. Never again in history would a Canadian Scottish battalion be piped into an attack.[22]

The Reckoning

The Dieppe raid cost almost four thousand Canadians and British killed, wounded, or captured. Able and enterprising Canadian correspondents sent back full reports of the raid, which newspapers and radio transmitted to the Canadian public, but British and American reports focused almost entirely on their own troops, with scarcely a mention of Canadian participation. Brigadier Denis Whitaker, the only Royal Hamilton officer to return to England, later wrote bitterly about a cover-up. Churchill and the Chiefs of Combined Operations did their best to deflect public criticism, particularly condemnation from Canada. Churchill, in particular, feigned ignorance and did his best to elude responsibility. Then, in writing his memoir of Dieppe, *Hinge of Fate*, Churchill finally backed down and assumed some of the blame:[23]

> [E]xtraordinary steps were taken to ensure secrecy. For this reason no records were kept but, after the Canadian authorities and the Chiefs of Staff had given their approval, I personally went through the plans with C.I.G.S., Admiral Mountbatten, and the Naval Force Commander, Captain J. Hughes-Hallet. It was clear no substantial change between "Jubilee" and "Rutter" was suggested, beyond substituting Commandos to silence Flank Coastal Batteries in place of airborne troops.[24]

Although Mountbatten had accepted arguments for the frontal attack, he had also suggested that they open with a preliminary aerial bombardment, that a battleship should be available for artillery support, and that marines and commandos should make up the assault force, rather than Canadians with no experience of an amphibious landing. None of these suggestions was included in the final plan.[25] Nevertheless, Mountbatten, as Chief of Combined Ops, became the principal figure of blame for the deaths of so many young Canadians,[26] although one American correspondent unfairly blamed General McNaughton for the raid's poor planning.[27] The official Canadian scapegoat, however, was General Hamilton Roberts. Although awarded the Distinguished Service Order (DSO)[28] for the operation, he lost his division and never again commanded troops in the field.[29]

> Churchill later wrote that valuable lessons were learned at Dieppe, that the Canadians had not died in vain. But the British chiefs should not have needed a debacle like Dieppe to learn the lessons; they were paid to plan not experiment. . . . Montgomery bore no responsibility for Dieppe, and Mountbatten escaped taking any. But [press baron, Lord] Beaverbrook took the slaughter of his fellow Canadians hard, and for the remainder of his life loathed Dickie Mountbatten.[30]

Getting to the Cemeteries and Memorials

In the months leading up to the raid on Dieppe, inevitably some soldiers died in accidents while training. At Dieppe, over five hundred soldiers died on the beaches or in the town; others made it back to England but subsequently died of wounds. Two hundred and eighty-eight soldiers were buried at **Brookwood Cemetery**, in Surrey, from the beginning of 1942, when training began, until the end of August. In all, the cemetery is the last resting place for 2,403 Canadians who died on British soil in the course of World War II. Two hundred more with no known grave are remembered on the Brookwood Memorial.

Brookwood Canadian Memorial

By train: Take the Basingstoke train from London Waterloo Station, which runs almost hourly with regular stops at Brookwood. The trip takes forty minutes with one change. From Brookwood Station, the cemetery is a ten-minute walk, about 650 metres, along Pine Avenue.

Left: Brookwood Cemetery, Surrey, England. Canadian Reception and Records Building. (Susan Evans Shaw)

Below: Brookwood Cemetery, Canadian Section. (Susan Evans Shaw)

By car: From nearby Aldershot, the place where Canadian troops were based during the war, head southeast on A323 (High Street) toward Victoria Road. Go through four roundabouts, then take a slight left onto Pirbright Road (A324). After two roundabouts, turn right opposite Pemberton Villa. Four hundred metres farther along, turn left to the cemetery entrance. The distance from Aldershot is about twelve kilometres.

Dieppe Canadian War Cemetery

Of the men who died at Dieppe, 538 are buried in the Dieppe Canadian War Cemetery at Hautot-sur-Mer, Seine-Maritime.

By car: From Dieppe Centre, take avenue Léon Gambetta (D925) to the first traffic circle, then take the second exit onto N27 (avenue des Canadiens) to the next traffic circle, where you will see a CWGC sign pointing the way. Exit onto rue des Canadiens. Across the intersection

Hautot-sur-Mer, Dieppe Canadian War Cemetery.
(Commonwealth War Graves Commission)

with chemin des Jonquilles, avenue des Canadiens becomes rue des Canarderies. From rue des Canarderies, turn left onto an unpaved sliproad to the cemetery; the entrance is in the wall to your left. The distance is about six kilometres.

St-Sever Cemetery Extension

Twenty-seven Canadians who took part in the Dieppe raid and died later of wounds are buried in the St-Sever Cemetery Extension, near Rouen.

By car: From the Dieppe Canadian War Cemetery, return to the N27 and continue south for about thirty-one kilometres. At the roundabout, continue on A151 for eighteen kilometres, merge onto A150 for eight kilometres, then continue onto N1338. At the roundabout, take the second exit and stay on N1338. At the next roundabout, take the fourth exit onto

St-Sever Cemetery near Rouen.
(Commonwealth War Graves Commission)

Bernières-sur-Mer, Normandy. The original Atlantic Wall was about five metres high but continuous wave action over the years has deposited sand so the exposed wall is currently less than one metre in height. (Susan Evans Shaw)

N338. Turn right onto avenue Jean Rondeaux. After three kilometres, turn right onto rue Pierre Lefrançois. The cemetery is on the right.

No visit to Dieppe is complete without a visit to the pebble beach and a close-up view of the Atlantic Wall. In the decades since the Canadian landing, wave action has increased the depth of the shingle. The original Atlantic Wall stood about five metres in height but is now just over a metre high; the rest is buried by shingle. A stroll on the beach is sufficient to give the experience of what the landing soldiers had to contend with underfoot.

From a lookout on the top of the cliff at the end of boulevard de la Mer and adjacent to the Château de Dieppe, there is a panoramic view of the beach and town. Few of the original buildings remain, but the vulnerability of the troops landing on the beach is apparent.

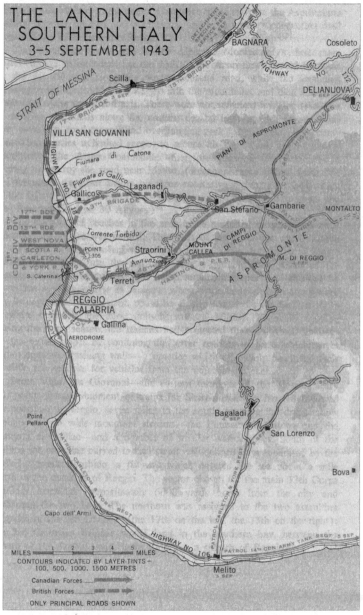

THE LANDINGS IN SOUTHERN ITALY
3–5 SEPTEMBER 1943

BAGNARA

Cosoleto

STRAIT OF MESSINA

Scilla

DELIANUOVA

HIGHWAY NO. 112

VILLA SAN GIOVANNI

Fiumara di Catona

PIANI DI ASPROMONTE

MONTALTO

Fiumara di Gallico

Laganadi

Gallico

San Stefano

Gambarie

Torrente Torbido

CAMPI DI REGGIO

MOUNT CALLEA

M. DI REGGIO

Straorini

ASPROMONTE

dell' Annunziata

Terreti

S. Caterina

REGGIO CALABRIA

Gallina

AERODROME

Point Pellaro

Bagaladi

San Lorenzo

Bova

Capo dell' Armi

HIGHWAY NO. 106

Melito

MILES 1 2 3 4 5 MILES

CONTOURS INDICATED BY LAYER-TINTS —
100, 500, 1000, 1500 METRES

Canadian Forces

British Forces

ONLY PRINCIPAL ROADS SHOWN

Source: G.W.L. Nicholson, *Official History of the Canadian Army in the Second World War. Volume II: The Canadians in Italy, 1943-1945* (Ottawa: Queen's Printer, 1966), map 6.

Part IV
The Canadians in Italy

The war in Italy was cruel and dirty. Under-equipped with everything but spirits, guts, and determination, the Canadians made a reputation as tough and courageous fighters. They slugged victoriously northward against an implacable, efficient, and seasoned enemy army, through the most difficult and heartbreaking terrain encountered by any army in the Second World War.[1]

By early 1943 the fortunes of war were turning against Germany, but instead of elation, discord reigned among the Allies, threatening unity. Disagreement between Churchill and Roosevelt hinged on the timing of an invasion of Europe. Whereas American doctrine favoured direct confrontation with the enemy, the British, haunted by the memory of the bloodbath that was the Western Front in the Great War, dreaded the high human cost of an invasion. Churchill preferred to take advantage of Britain's naval superiority to chip away at the periphery of Occupied Europe.[2]

Eager as they were for a fight, the American troops lacked the experience necessary to tackle a full-scale assault against the well-trained German Army and the fortress that constituted the French coastal defences. The need for action convinced Roosevelt to commit his forces in November 1942 to an invasion of Northwest Africa. If nothing else, the American troops would gain by the experience of warfare.

While the rest of the world warred, Canadian troops continued to train in England.[3] Except for the tragic fiasco that was Dieppe, Canadians had taken little part in the war, and Prime Minister Mackenzie King preferred it that way. His primary concern remained fixed on the need to preserve Canadian lives, avoid conscription, and avert a political crisis. If that meant keeping the Canadians out of combat, then so be it.

Canadian military did not share the prime minister's fears. Memory of the Canadian Expeditionary Force's distinguished performance in the Great War remained fresh enough that Canada's present idleness in the circumstances was considered a national disgrace. Mounting public pressure eventually made Mackenzie King realize that Canadians could not be kept out of the action any longer. But rather than face the possibility of heavy casualties in another cross-Channel invasion, he agreed to the deployment of at least part of the Canadian Army elsewhere, in the hope that casualties would be slight.

The Soft Underbelly of Europe

At the conclusion of the Casablanca Conference in January 1943, Churchill's plan to attack the "soft underbelly of Europe" by striking at Germany's Axis partner, Italy, prevailed over Roosevelt's insistence on an immediate cross-Channel invasion.[4] That invasion certainly would take place, but not yet. For one thing, the Allies were insufficiently trained for the undertaking, and an invasion of Italy could be a way to instil the troops with essential skills. To reinforce the argument, Churchill noted that, if Italy were pushed out of the war, Germany would be forced to replace Italian divisions with German troops, further diluting Hitler's already diminished strength.

Operation Husky, as conceived in July 1943, had three goals: to secure the Mediterranean line of communication; to redirect German forces from the Russian front; and to intensify pressure on Italy. American general Dwight Eisenhower was chosen commander-in-chief of the whole operation. The Western Task Force would consist of the American Seventh Army, commanded by General Mark Clark, and the British Eighth Army, under General Montgomery. The combined force would assault the southeastern coast of Sicily in an amphibious landing. American forces would land at the port of Licata, the assault area farthest to the west.[5] Montgomery's Eighth Army would assault with two corps, consisting of a total of six infantry divisions, one infantry brigade, and one airborne division.[6] Late in the planning, the Canadians accepted an invitation to serve with the Eighth Army.[7]

As far as Canadian commander Major-General Andy McNaughton was concerned, the Sicilian operation would be valuable experience for his troops and a change from the endless drills and training in England. Following the costly debacle of Dieppe, the 2nd Canadian Division still faced a long and hard period of recovery. Thus, in what turned out to be a wise decision, McNaughton selected the 1st Canadian Division and the 1st Canadian Army Tank Brigade to head for the Mediterranean. The nine infantry battalions included the Princess Patricia's Canadian Light Infantry (PPCLI), the Royal Canadian Regiment (RCR), the Royal 22e Régiment (Van Doos), the Saskatoon Light Infantry, the Hastings and Prince Edward Regiment (Hasty Ps), the 48th Highlanders of Canada, the Seaforth Highlanders of Canada, the Loyal Edmonton Regiment (Loyal Eddies), the Carlton and York Regiment, and the West Nova Scotia Regiment (the Westies). The 1st Canadian Tank Brigade of three units contained the only formation with battle experience, the Calgary Regiment (Calgary Tanks) having served at Dieppe. The other two units were the Ontario Regiment and the Three Rivers Regiment. Major-General Guy Granville Simonds, at forty Canada's youngest general officer, took command of the Canadian force following the death in a plane crash of General Harry Salmon, its original commanding officer.

The Canadian troops were shipped from England first to Scotland for advanced training near Inverary, where they were re-equipped with Tommy guns and Projector, Infantry, Anti-Tank (PIAT) weapons, amphibious trucks (DUKW), and the new Sherman tank. The tank crews, mostly farmers and ranchers from southern Alberta accustomed to heavy vehicles, had no problem adapting to driving the Shermans.[8]

Left: Sherman tank.
(CWM 19990009-001 © Canadian War Museum)

Below: DUKW, amphibious truck.
(CWM 19970113-012 © Canadian War Museum)

THE SICILIAN CAMPAIGN
Sweltering Heat and Clouds of Flies

> Trudging great distances over Scottish bogs was tough, but not
> as tough as marching twenty miles in a broiling Sicilian sun after
> a sleepless night and then going into action, perhaps without a
> meal. . . . That the division successfully rose to the occasion of
> an assault landing followed by arduous fighting after two weeks
> cooped up in ships on a long sea voyage is a remarkable testament
> to Canadian grit, planning and training.[9]

More than eighteen hundred Canadian officers and twenty-five thousand
other ranks plus thirty thousand tons of supplies sailed from the River
Clyde on June 28, 1943, along with headquarters ship HMS *Hilary*,

a former passenger liner, from which the assault would be directed. Their destination was Sicily, an island roughly the shape of a triangle off the toe of the Italian boot. Landing on July 10 at two sandy beaches at Costa dell'Ambra on the southeastern coast, the Canadians met with difficulties caused by weather and sandbars. Opposition from the Italian military, however, was negligible; with no heart for a fight, Italian soldiers surrendered in droves, only too happy to be out of the conflict. Pachino airfield, a few kilometres from the landing beaches, was the first objective assigned the Canadians. The RCR arrived at the airfield unopposed and found the place deserted, although the runways were heavily damaged.

Nonetheless, as the invasion moved inland, Sicily's rugged mountainous countryside gave the advantage to the German defenders, who were determined to fight on despite the defection of their Italian allies. From strongholds above the mountain passes and narrow roads, they used mortars, machine-gun fire, and deadly sniping to impede the Canadians' progress. Undeterred, village by village the Canadians pushed on through the dust and heat. Battling their way across country, they gradually subdued the Germans and captured in rapid succession the towns of Vizzini, Grammichele, Caltagirone, Piazza Armerina, and Valguarnera.

The next objective presented the Canadians with a tough obstacle. High above the Leonforte-Assoro passage through the mountains and garrisoned by the formidable 15th Panzer Grenadier Division, the village of Assoro guarded the route to Catania and the coast. A frontal attack would have been suicidal. Instead five hundred infantrymen of

General Bernard Montgomery at Pachino Beach (The Royal Canadian Regiment, The RCR Museum, Wolseley Barracks, London, ON)

SICILY
10 JULY – 17 AUGUST, 1943

MILES 10 5 0 10 20 30 40 50 MILES

LEGEND

Ground over 200 metres above sea level	
Ground over 600 metres above sea level	
Ground over 1000 metres above sea level	
Ground over 1400 metres above sea level	

ONLY PRINCIPAL ROADS SHOWN

Canadian Forces
British Forces
United States Forces

ONLY MAIN LINES OF ADVANCE OF NON-CANADIAN FORMATIONS ARE SHOWN

HIGHWAY NOS. INDICATED THUS 117

Map labels: PALERMO 22 JUL, TRAPANI 23 JUL, Castellammare, Alcamo, Campofelice, Termini Imerese 23 JUL, Marsala, CORLEONE, Castelvetrano 21 JUL, Sciacca 20 JUL, CALTANISS..., AGRIGENTO 17 JUL, Porto Empedocle, Palma di Montechiaro, Licata, 2ND ARMOURED DIVISION, 3rd DIVISION, 82ND AIRBORNE DIV, PROVISIONAL CORPS, 45TH

Source: G.W.L. Nicholson, *Official History of the Canadian Army in the Second World War. Volume II: The Canadians in Italy, 1943-1945* (Ottawa: Queen's Printer, 1966), map 1.

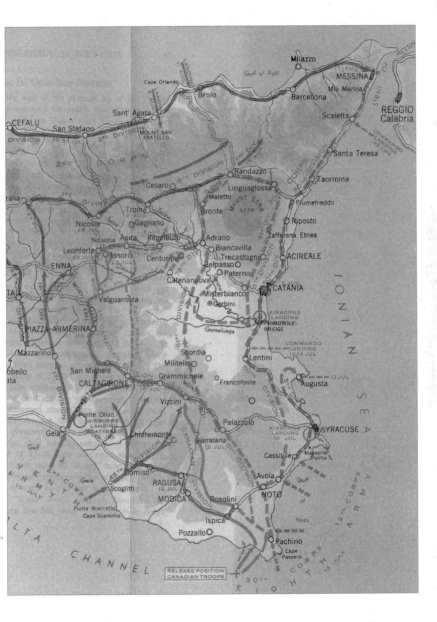

the Hasty Ps, hauling guns and a radio set, achieved the impossible by scaling a three-hundred-metre cliff behind the village.[10] The enemy was taken completely by surprise. From their vantage point on the crest of the mountain, the Canadians opened fire and, using the radio, directed gunners below where to fire shells and mortars. With pinpoint accuracy, they destroyed the blockade and enemy tanks.[11] The Germans retreated to Nissoria, where the Canadians next faced a head-on counterattack by a furious and vengeful force. The Canadians triumphed, however, after a bitter fight, and cleared the Germans from the town before pushing on to yet another hard fight at Agira.

The Red Patches Are Devils

"Red Patches just keep coming through the fire. . . . Other troops we fought lay down and took shelter when the mortars fired right on top of them. The Red Patches are devils." A German officer commenting in a press interview. [12]

A few kilometres to the south, at Catenanuova, the Third Brigade got a welcome surprise when, in an unusual case of German cowardice, the defenders fled without a fight. A furious General Field Marshal Wilhelm Keitel initiated court martial proceedings against the officers responsible for the cowardly flight.[13] The Canadians' reputation as tough combatants had grown with each battle, but nevertheless they had to be faced.

In a smoothly planned action, the Canadians took the town of Regalbuto. After crossing the River Simeto without bloodshed on the night of August 5, Adrano became their final stop. As the Allies closed on Messina, the battle front constricted so that some formations could be taken out for a rest. Twenty days of non-stop fighting had certainly blooded the Canadian troops; at last they could feel they had lived up to the reputation won by their fathers in the Great War. Montgomery awarded them a well-deserved rest in an area at Militello, near the southern edge of the Catania plain.[14] Entertainment was laid on for the troops, but there was also a tightening of discipline in matters of dress and saluting, particularly unpopular with the men after the laxity of rules as they battled across Sicily.[15]

While the Eighth Army was battling its way to Messina across the eastern portion of Sicily, the American Seventh Army, under command of the ever-competitive General George Patton, landed farther west along the Sicilian coast. Marching to the north of the island, they made a triumphant entry into the Sicilian capital of Palermo. The victorious Patton established himself in the Royal Palace, where he drank champagne and ate K-rations off crested porcelain in the state dining room.[16] Patton's capture of Palermo made for good press, but delayed by several days the more critical American drive toward Messina.[17] Even more significantly, it allowed the Germans time for a highly efficient move of forty thousand troops, along with guns, tanks, vehicles, and tons of ammunition, across the Strait of Messina to the mainland. Patton and the Seventh Army arrived at Messina before Montgomery's Eighth Army, but to no purpose — the Germans had already escaped.[18]

Getting to the Cemeteries and Memorials

Agira Canadian War Cemetery (pp. 76-77) is in the centre of Sicily, roughly equidistant from Palermo, Messina, and Pachino, and 5 kilometres from the town of Agira. Of the 490 burials, 484 are Canadian.

By car: From Agira, head north on Via Vittorio Emanuele to Via Santa Maria di Gesù and turn right. At the roundabout take the first exit onto SS121, which follows a tortuous route for just over four kilometres. At a fork in the road, take the right. The steeply terraced cemetery is two hundred metres on the left.

Catania War Cemetery (p. 74) is about eight kilometres south of Catania, on the east coast of Sicily and under the still-active volcano of Mount Etna. Of the 2,022 identified Commonwealth burials, only 13 are Canadian, all but one airmen with the RCAF. The lone Canadian infantryman is Lieutenant George Redvers Hudson Banks Stewart, of the Black Watch (Royal Highland Regiment) of Canada, age twenty-two.[19]

By car: Head south from Catania on the Via Acquicella Porto to the Via Priolo Sopraelevata, and continue for 2.1 kilometres to the SP701. After 1.9 kilometres, take the ramp to Enna. At the roundabout, take the second exit to Via Paseo del Fico. Catania War Cemetery is 900 metres on the right. Because of littering and vandalism, access to the cemetery is controlled by a gate 500 metres from the cemetery, which is kept locked with a padlock; the combination is 1221. Outside the gardeners' normal working hours, the Visitors Book and Registers are kept locked in the gardeners' tool shed. Consult the CWGC website for exact hours.[20]

Syracuse War Cemetery is located three kilometres west of Syracuse, an ancient coastal city about fifty kilometres south of Catania. Of the more than one thousand burials here, only two are Canadian, both airmen with the RCAF.

By car: Take the Corso Gelone on the western fringe of the city, a distance of about three kilometres. At the roundabout beside the archaeological park, take the first exit onto Viale Paolo Orsi. Continue onto Viale Ermocrate/SS124. Keep on SS124 for 1.2 kilometres. Syracuse War Cemetery is on the right.

THE ITALIAN CAMPAIGN
The Spaghetti League

> The Regiment embarked in its landing craft at noon on September
> 3, and enjoyed a pleasant outing on a pleasant sea. For spice
> there were seven Fiat fighter [aircraft] that swept in from the
> east, danced prettily in the sky some miles away, dropped their
> bombs where they would do no harm, and flew off content with
> their gesture of defiance. The landing craft nosed into the Italian
> beaches and there were no difficulties to contend with other than
> heat, thirst, and overloaded haversacks.[21]

At dawn on September 3, 1943, the fourth anniversary of Britain's declaration of war, the Canadians crossed the Strait of Messina and waded ashore on the Italian mainland, becoming the first Allied troops to return to and remain on the continent since the British were driven out of France three years earlier. Remembering the humiliation of Dunkirk, the mood of the Allied forces this day was exultant.

The landing was unopposed. The beaches were deserted: no mines, no barbed wire, no defenders. Everywhere, Italian coastal defence troops surrendered.[22] In fact, the British-Canadian landings on the toe of Italy were intended only as a feint to distract German attention from the landing of the American Fifth Army farther north, at Salerno, the idea being to trap the German divisions in the south as they concentrated their forces on the British Eighth Army.[23] But the Germans foresaw a trap, and remained in the north. Reinforced by thirty thousand troops successfully transferred from Sardinia and Corsica and reorganized as the 90th Panzer Grenadier Division, they counterattacked at Salerno and threatened to drive the Americans back into the sea.

In the south, the Canadians took the town of Reggio di Calabria and its airfield from local Italian forces without a fight.[24] Then, leaving behind the sweltering heat and flies of the coast, they set out for the cool,

mist-shrouded terraces of the Aspromonte plateau. An easy march for the first eight kilometres ended abruptly when the Canadians began to encounter German-made obstacles—blown bridges and deep craters in the road. But the engineers, unsung heroes of the march, laboured non-stop to eliminate each and every obstruction.

The first clash with the enemy took place on September 4 at Gambarie, a ski resort on the plateau about twenty kilometres inland. There, the 48th Highlanders came face to face with troops of the Italian Fascist militia, the Black Shirts. In the ensuing battle, nine Black Shirts were killed and thirty were captured, along with field artillery, machine guns, and two hundred folding bicycles. A few days later, at Cittanova, the Loyal Eddies, travelling overland from the east, and the PPCLI, from the west, clashed with Italian paratroopers, neither side aware that Italy had surrendered that very day.[25]

From Cittanova, the Canadians headed for the Adriatic coast, then moved rapidly north, barely hindered by German booby traps and other obstacles. Through Catanzaro, Crotone, Villapiana, and Rotondella, their trajectory turned inland toward the key road and rail centre of Potenza, a place of fine churches and sun-bleached buildings situated on an eight-hundred-metre height of land overlooking the River Basenta.[26] Despite having to contend with destroyed bridges, the Canadians' progress was so speedy that they took the Germans in Potenza—a hundred paratroopers well equipped with automatic weapons—by surprise. The Van Doos were called in to help, but by the time they arrived, the Germans had fled.

In the course of the rapid six-hundred-kilometre advance from Reggio, casualties had been light, but the sickness toll was alarming.[27] Fifteen hundred soldiers were stricken with malaria and infectious jaundice, including Major-General Guy Simonds, who was evacuated to hospital at Bari. The colourful, fiery, but humane Chris Vokes was promoted to major-general, and took charge as Simonds's replacement.

Meanwhile, Hitler, infuriated by the Allied invasion of the Italian mainland and Italy's capitulation, ordered that swift advantage be taken of the surrender. German forces seized control of the country and disarmed the Italian soldiers, who would be used as forced labour. Hitler then appointed the very capable Field Marshal Albert Kesselring supreme commander of German forces in Italy, and reassigned his favourite, Field Marshal Erwin Rommel, to Northwest Europe in anticipation of an invasion there.

Among the Allies, disorder ruled. They had now landed large numbers of troops in Italy, but as yet they had come up with no overall strategic plan as to what to do with them. Nobody seemed to know why they were in Italy except to knock the Italians out of the war. Nonetheless, Mackenzie King approved the release of another Canadian division to serve in Italy. The Canadian Army would now be split: one corps would remain in Britain to continue training for the forthcoming invasion of France, while the other corps would fight in Italy. According to the long-term plan, the two corps would unite when the troops from Italy invaded through the south of France.

Getting to the Cemeteries and Memorials

Bari War Cemetery is located on the outskirts of Bari, a city on the Adriatic coast in the locality of Carbonara. There was never any serious fighting at Bari, but it was an important supply base and hospital centre. After the war, burials from around the area were brought in to the cemetery, which is also the burial place of naval men killed in two explosions of ammunition ships in the harbour, one in December 1943 during a German air raid and the second in April 1945.[28] There are 2,128 Commonwealth burials of World War II in the cemetery, including 210 Canadians and 170 unidentified. Eighty-five World War I burials were brought in from Brindisi in 1981, one of whom, William Gilbert, was a seaman of the Newfoundland Royal Naval Reserve.

By car: From E55/SS16 ring road around Bari, take exit 13A to SS100 southbound. From SS100 take the exit toward Bari Carbonara and turn left onto SP135. Continue onto SP144, and the Bari War Cemetery is on the right. Like so many Commonwealth war cemeteries of World War II, this is a neat rectangle in the middle of farmland—in this case vineyards. The Stone of Remembrance at the entrance is flanked by two white cloister-like structures, one of which houses the Register and Visitors Book.

Italy, Bari War Cemetery. The Stone of Remembrance at the entrance is flanked by two white cloister-like structures, one of which houses the Register and Visitors Book.
(Commonwealth War Graves Commission)

Italy, Salerno War Cemetery. Visible to the east are the mountains of the natural preserve Parco regionale Monti Picentini. (Commonwealth War Graves Commission)

Salerno War Cemetery is located twenty kilometres southeast of Salerno. There are 1,846 Commonwealth burials here, including 27 Canadians and 107 unidentified.

By car: From Salerno, take the A3/E45 toward Reggio/Caserta/Bari/Aeroporto and travel 17.5 kilometres to the exit for Montecorvino/Pontecagnano Sud/Aeroporto. At the roundabout, take the first exit onto Via Antonio Vivaldi to a T-intersection. Turn left onto SS18. A CWGC sign indicates the way to Salerno War Cemetery, which is one kilometre on the left.

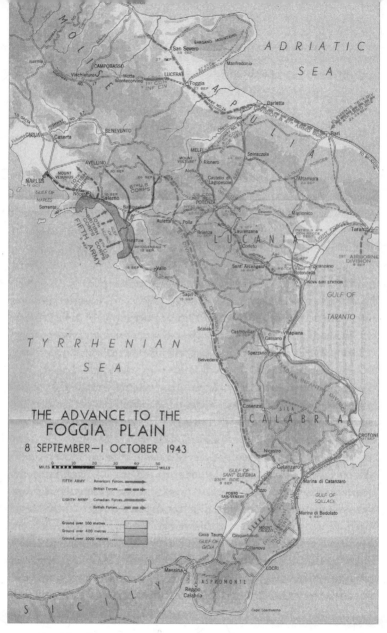

THE ADVANCE TO THE
FOGGIA PLAIN
8 SEPTEMBER—1 OCTOBER 1943

| MILES | 0 | 10 | 20 | 30 | 40 | 50 | MILES |

FIFTH ARMY   American Forces
              British Forces
EIGHTH ARMY   Canadian Forces
              British Forces

Ground over 100 metres
Ground over 400 metres
Ground over 1000 metres

Source: G.W.L. Nicholson, *Official History of the Canadian Army in the Second World War. Volume II: The Canadians in Italy, 1943-1945* (Ottawa: Queen's Printer, 1966), map 8.

Monty's Mountain Goats

> The German strategy had so far been to conduct a slow, carefully controlled withdrawal up Italy's boot. . . . To break through whichever German line they faced at the particular moment, the Allies had to deploy their forces and prepare a major offensive operation. When the assault went in, the Germans would usually only hold for a very brief time before retreating in good order to a new well-prepared defensive line. This strategy slowed the Allied advance to a crawl. It also assured that German casualties and loss of precious war materiel remained tolerably low. The opposite was true for Allied forces. Losses absorbed were always out of proportion to ground gained.[29]

At the beginning of October, following the rest break at Potenza, the Canadians moved toward their next objective, Campobasso, nestled in the Apennine foothills west of the Foggia plain. Their route took them north to Canosa and Foggia. Along the way, at Motta Montecorvino, a company of RCRs outflanked the enemy's defences and the Germans pulled out before they could be surrounded. But new and effective enemy delaying tactics, and skirmishes with the 29th Panzer Grenadier Division at Gambalesa, Toppo Fornelli, Jelsi, and Gildone, slowed up the Canadians' arrival at Campobasso. Even so, by the middle of October they got to within striking distance of the city, where an alerted enemy waited. The city had served as Field Marshal Kesselring's headquarters, and an assault required careful planning. As well, the Canadians were tired, so the attack was delayed until the morning. But it all came to nothing. The Panzer Grenadiers pulled out without firing a shot, although they later claimed they had fought a hard battle before withdrawing.[30]

From Campobasso, the Canadians consolidated their position on the east bank of the Biferno River and proceeded to harass German outposts in an attempt to pry them out of their holdings on the far side. Sporadic fighting delayed any Canadian advance until the Germans could complete a withdrawal across the Sangro River to defences behind the Bernhard Line. With typical Teutonic thoroughness, the Germans left behind a trail of devastation as they destroyed roads and bridges and swept the countryside in a scorched earth campaign. In their wake, unflagging Canadian engineers scored a triumph by reconstructing those same bridges and roads, including one fifty-five-metre span, a feat that was accomplished in just eighteen hours.[31] The operation completed, the Canadians left for Ortona and the bloodiest month of the whole Italian campaign.

The Battle of Ortona

Since July 10, 1st Canadian Infantry Division and 1st Canadian Armoured Division had been on campaign. Five months of fighting and marching. Moments of terror and horror interspersed with extended periods of boredom and the drudgery of the advance across Sicily and up Italy's boot.[32]

Ortona, a small town of ten thousand on the Adriatic coast, was a popular vacation spot for industrial and factory workers from the north, a place to escape the blistering summer heat of Rome and other cities. The harbour had been formed by the construction of two moles, like pincers at either end of Ortona's natural bay. Built of rock and earth, the moles sheltered the harbour from storms and prevented silt from filling up the basin, creating one of the few deepwater ports on the Adriatic coast. South of the harbour stretched a beautiful white sand beach where holidaymakers would congregate in large family groups to enjoy sea and sun.

German soldiers arrived in Ortona on September 24, 1943, and immediately took control of the port and proceeded to make the harbour inaccessible to sea-going vessels by cutting through the moles at more than a dozen places. Within weeks the port became too shallow to permit any

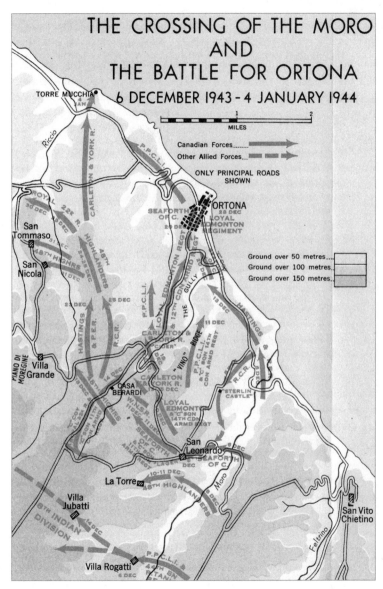

THE CROSSING OF THE MORO
AND
THE BATTLE FOR ORTONA
6 DECEMBER 1943 - 4 JANUARY 1944

MILES

Canadian Forces........
Other Allied Forces........

ONLY PRINCIPAL ROADS
SHOWN

Ground over 50 metres....
Ground over 100 metres....
Ground over 150 metres....

TORRE MUCCHIA

ORTONA

San Tommaso

San Nicola

Villa Grande

CASA BERARDI

"VINO" RIDGE

"STERLIN CASTLE"

San Leonardo

La Torre

Villa Jubatti

8TH INDIAN DIVISION

Villa Rogatti

San Vito Chietino

SEAFORTH OF C.

LOYAL EDMONTON REGIMENT

Source: G.W.L. Nicholson, *Official History of the Canadian Army in the Second World War.*
Volume II: The Canadians in Italy, 1943-1945 (Ottawa: Queen's Printer, 1966), map 11,
inset.

kind of shipping. Larger boats in the harbour were sunk and fishermen were forbidden to go to sea. An attempt was made to dragoon local Italians as free labour, but the townsmen had no sympathy with the Fascists and, fearing the dreaded SS squads, managed to elude German recruiters.[33]

For the Allies, it would be a tough winter of fighting in rough terrain. Enemy troops and tanks poured into Italy, which well suited the Allied objective of draining German forces away from Northwest Europe. The immediate Allied goal, however, was to pierce the Bernhard and Gustav Lines, the German winter defensive positions, and get across the Moro River as soon as possible. Despite the damage to Ortona's port, capturing the town and repairing its facilities would shorten lines of supply to Allied divisions as they moved north.

The Canadians' attack on Ortona was led by divisional commander Chris Vokes. The battle, notable for both brutality and small acts of humanity, lasted twenty-eight days and left the town in ruins. A triumphant General Vokes reported: "We smashed the 90th Panzer Grenadier Division and we gave the 1st German Parachute Division a mauling which it will long remember."[34] But the price had been high, and Vokes was held responsible for the heavy losses, although it was Montgomery who insisted on prolonging the operation in impossible ground and weather conditions.

For many of the Canadians, Christmas 1943 was their fifth away from home and family. Battalion quartermasters made an extra effort to see that the day was not overlooked. A Christmas dinner was prepared and served in a village church behind the lines. One company at a time, the men trooped to the rear and sat down to a meal of soup, a roast, a vegetable, mashed potatoes, and gravy, Christmas pudding, and mince pies. After a two-hour respite, the men returned to battle.[35]

The last action of the campaign was fought on January 4, 1944, at Point 59, overlooking Torre Mucchia. Two German strongpoints were taken, and the Canadians secured their line along the Riccio River.

The Eighth Army then reduced its pressure on the enemy and began a transition to static warfare.

From the Moro River through Ortona, the Canadians counted 695 dead, 1,738 wounded, and 1,773 sick. Nevertheless, in the three months following the launch of Operation Husky, the Allies had captured Sicily, seen Italy knocked out of the war, and obtained the airfields of Foggia and Naples for further action against the German enemy.

Getting to the Cemeteries and Memorials

Moro River Canadian War Cemetery is approximately 3 kilometres from the centre of Ortona, on the Adriatic coast. Of the more than 1,600 burials here, 1,357 are of Canadians killed in the battle for Ortona and the Moro River. The cemetery is an almost perfect square enclosed by a hedge and surrounded by olive groves. Past the Stone of Remembrance at the entryway, a stone path leads straight to the Cross of Sacrifice at the centre of an inner square.

By car: Head south from Ortona on Corso Vittorio Emanuele toward Porta Calderi and continue straight onto Via Della Liberta for five hundred metres. Turn left onto Viale Margherita d'Austria, which makes a hairpin descent from the town. At the bottom, turn left onto Strada Statale 16 Adriatica and continue for 1.7 kilometres, then make a sharp left toward the church of San Donato, which stands just before the entrance to the cemetery.

Caserta War Cemetery (p. 74) occupies a section of Caserta Communal Cemetery. At Caserta, thirty-six kilometres north of Naples, 2nd General Hospital and two Canadian military hospitals were set up in late 1943 and served until the end of the war. Of the more than seven hundred burials here, ninety-nine are Canadian. Burials include those who died in the hospitals as well as prisoners from a nearby prisoner-of-war camp.

By car: From Naples, take the A3 for 3 kilometres to the exit onto toll road A1/E45, direction Caserta/Roma/Avellino/Aeroporto. Continue north for 28 kilometres to exit Caserta Nord, another toll road. Turn left onto SS7/Via Nazionale Appia for 1.3 kilometres, then turn left onto Via Passionisti to Via Col. Michele Camusso. Turn right and continue straight ahead for about 1.5 kilometres to Via Cappucini and turn left. At the roundabout, take the first exit onto Via Gen. Luigi Tatamonti. Caserta War Cemetery is 200 metres on the left.

Naples War Cemetery was established in late 1943 to serve three general hospitals and a garrison located in the city. Shallow marble steps lead to the entrance between marble columns. The Register and Visitors Book are housed on the right. The Cross of Sacrifice at the rear of the cemetery is flanked by two austere classical structures of white marble, lending an air of quiet serenity to the landscape. Burials include graves moved from smaller cemeteries in the immediate district. Of the 1,202 Commonwealth burials, 39 are Canadian.

By car: From Piazza Guiseppe Garibaldi in the heart of Naples, take the first right onto Via Cesare Rosaroll. After one kilometre, turn left onto Via Foria. Continue straight on to Piazza Camillo Benso Conte di Cavour, then to Piazza Museo Nazionale. Take the next right onto Via S. Teresa degli Scalzi, which becomes Corso Amedeo di Savoia Duca D'Aosta. Turn right onto Tondo di Capodimonte to Via Capodimonto, a road that twists in switchbacks until it ends at Via Miano. Turn left, and after one kilometre turn left again onto Via Nuova S. Rocco. Continue for eight hundred metres, then turn right onto Via Raffaele Marfella. After another eight hundred metres, turn right onto Via Vincenzo Janfolla. Naples War Cemetery is 280 metres on the right.

Ortona from the sea. (RaBoe / Wikipedia / Wikimedia Commons / CC BY-SA 2.5)

Italy, Anzio, Entrance to the Beach Head War Cemetery. Facing opposite this cemetary is the Sicily-Rome American Cemetery and Memorial.

(Commonwealth War Graves Commission)

Italy, Minturno War Cemetery,
entrance marked by two pillars
topped by a lion on the left and
an eagle on the right. (Commonwealth
War Graves Commission)

Monte Cassino Arch-Abbey, restored.
(Ludmiła Pilecka / Wikimedia Commons / CC BY 3.0)

Left: Montecchio War Cemetery (Commonwealth War Graves Commission)

Above: Florence War Cemetery. The Cross of Sacrifice faces the entrance and a grassy avenue with Lombardy poplars leads to the Stone of Remembrance overlooking the River Arno. (Commonwealth War Graves Commission)

Facing page top: Foiana della Chiana War Cemetery surrounded by maize fields like those that concealed German panzers. (Commonwealth War Graves Commission)

Cesena War Cemetery
(Commonwealth War Graves Commission)

Above: Bagnacavallo, Italy, Villanova Canadian War Cemetery is a battlefield burial ground chosen by the 5th Canadian Armoured Division after heavy fighting at the River Lamone.

(Commonwealth War Graves Commission)

Source: G.W.L. Nicholson, *Official History of the Canadian Army in the Second World War. Volume II: The Canadians in Italy, 1943-1945* (Ottawa: Queen's Printer, 1966), back endpaper.

SWITZERLAN

Mila

Genoa

Nice

Cannes

Toulon

ILES D'HYÈRES

NORTHERN ITALY
10 JUNE 1944 – 25 FEBRUARY 1945

MILES 0   50   100 MILES

CORSICA

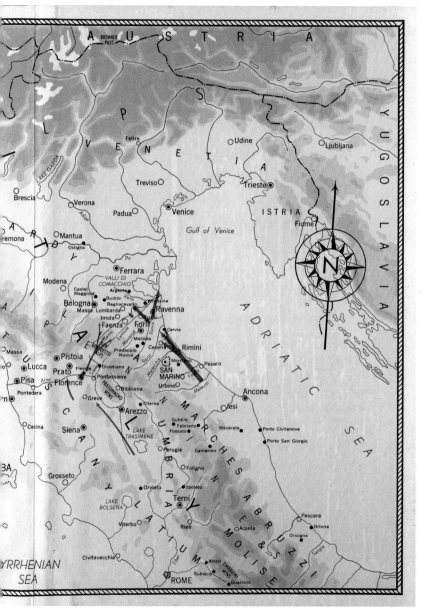

Above: Santerno Valley War Cemetery. (Commonwealth War Graves Commission)

Below: Argenta Gap Cemetery. (Commonwealth War Graves Commission)

THE ADRIATIC FRONT

Toward the end of 1943, Montgomery was withdrawn from Italy for a much-needed rest before the invasion of Northwest Europe, and Sir Oliver Leese took charge of Eighth Army. The winter saw a grim series of battles as the Allies tried to drive north and crack the German mountain and river defence lines.[36] The Canadians, now with General Harry Crerar in command after McNaughton's retirement, fought long and hard to clear the Germans from the high ground between the Riccio and Arielli rivers, west of Villa Grande. Time and again, huge volumes of artillery fire from the ridge forced them back while casualty rates soared. The Germans continued to hold in strength the approach to Tollo-Villa Grande as the Adriatic front settled in for the winter. The pause gave the Canadians a measure of relief after an extended period of intense fighting.[37] Stuck in a salient north of Ortona, General Crerar remarked on the similarity to Passchendaele in the 1914-1918 war. Surrounded by shattered farmhouses, burnt haystacks, shell-pocked fields befouled by unburied German dead, littered with equipment and burnt-out tanks, the troops slept, ate, and lived in cold slime. Endless rain saturated everything. Battledress became a clammy shroud and a stinking mush of sodden wool[38] as the two sides faced each other over the gully that became no-man's land. Crerar tried to revive a World War I Canadian specialty by ordering trench raids and aggressive patrols. These were carried out at considerable risk, but the chances of success were not good and the results unimpressive. The new generation of soldiers seemed to lack the hunting and stalking abilities of their fathers, and the patrols became destructive of morale and wasteful of manpower.

To everyone's relief, however, Crerar soon departed for Northwest Europe. His replacement, General E.L.M. (Tommy) Burns, "a very cold and austere personality,"[39] would lead the Canadians Corps for the next six months. As preparations for the Normandy invasion moved into high gear, officers serving in Italy were selected for service in Northwest Europe. Changes in command ensued as majors, captains, lieutenants, and senior NCOs departed for England.

Anzio Beach Disaster

On January 22, 1944, an American and a British division made an unopposed landing at Anzio, fifty-six kilometres south of Rome, their main object the capture of the Alban Hills south of the city.[40] Instead of moving his troops swiftly to their objective, however, American major-general John P. Lucas held them back from venturing inland while he consolidated his beachhead position. The delay gave the enemy time to assemble a devastating counterattack after effectively sealing off the beachhead. Reinforcements arrived, but instead of leading a triumphant march on Rome, they found themselves fighting a desperate defensive battle.[41]

The Canadian Special Service Battalion had a small but significant role to play at Anzio. As part of the Canadian-American First Special Service Force, they arrived at the beachhead at the beginning of February and set up headquarters in a farmhouse within twenty metres of the

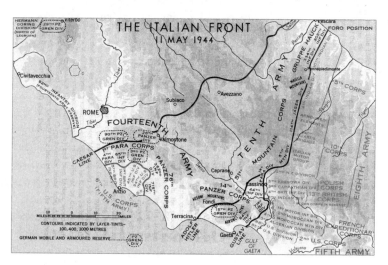

Source: Source: G.W.L. Nicholson, *Official History of the Canadian Army in the Second World War. Volume II: The Canadians in Italy, 1943-1945* (Ottawa: Queen's Printer, 1966), map 12.

front line. From there the battalion proceeded to make the enemy's life miserable with nightly patrols, attacking at opportune moments, always keeping the element of surprise. Sergeant Tommy Prince of Manitoba became the most successful of the raiders and the most decorated Canadian aboriginal soldier of the war, earning the Military Medal and the Silver Star. By the time the Special Force pulled out in May 9, 1944, losses numbered 384 killed, wounded, or missing, 117 of whom were Canadian.

Getting to the Cemeteries and Memorials

Anzio War Cemetery was established shortly after the beach landings in an area of Anzio adjacent to the communal cemetery. Nearly all of the 1,038 burials here are British, but there is one Canadian, Lieutenant Terry Faulkner Rowe, a cinematographer and member of the Army Film and Photo Unit.

Beach Head War Cemetery (p.113) is located close to what was once a casualty clearing station 4 kilometres north of the beaches at Anzio. Of the 2,025 identified Commonwealth burials, 68 are Canadian. On the west side of the road, facing the Commonwealth Cemetery, is the Sicily-Rome American Cemetery and Memorial.

By car: From Anzio, head south on SP601 and take the first left onto SP101b/Via Severiano. At the roundabout, take the third exit onto SR207/Via Nethunese. Continue through two roundabouts for 3.8 kilometres to the Beach Head War Cemetery on the right.

LIRI VALLEY
Gateway to Rome

> The battle to break into and through the Liri Valley lasted more
> than five months. Americans, British, Indians, New Zealanders,
> French, Poles, and Canadians all had their turn, as the fight
> escalated in size and intensity.[42]

After their defeat on the Adriatic front, the Germans retired to their next
defensive position, the Gustav Line. For 137 kilometres over the highest
peaks, the line crossed the Apennines from Ortona to the Gulf of Gaeta,
the narrow ankle of the Italian boot. The passage from the south to Rome,
the ancient Via Casilina perpetuated as Highway 6,[43] runs through the
Liri Valley, bordered on the north by the Matese Massif and on the
south by the coastal Aurunci Mountains. The Gustav Line blocked the
entrance to the valley, extending through the mountains north of Monte
Cassino to the coast at Gaeta. The Rapido, Gari, and Garigliano Rivers
form a natural barrier.

A monastery atop Monte Cassino overlooked the mouth of the Liri
Valley and strategically anchored the Gustav Line. Founded in 529 AD,
the monastery was destroyed successively in 581 by the Lombards, in 883
by the Saracens, in 1349 by an earthquake, and on February 15, 1944, by
Allied bombs. In the wake of the bombing, the German 1st Parachute
Division occupied the ruins and set up powerful defences. In response,
Field Marshal Earl Alexander, commander of the Allied Armies in Italy,
ordered a four-division battering ram. Divisions from the British XIII
Corps and the Polish Corps constituted the sledgehammer, code-named
Operation Diadem, to capture Monte Cassino and break the Gustav
Line. Held in reserve out of sight, the Canadian Corps would exploit
the breakthrough.

As in the Great War, the Germans had come to both admire and
fear Canadian soldiers for their resilience, tenacity, and courage as

Destroyed Monte Cassino Abbey, February 1944.
(Bundesarchiv, Bild 146-2005-0004 / Wittke / CC BY-SA 3.0)

fighters. Whenever and wherever they turned up, the Germans knew something major was underway, so the Canadians had to be transferred from the Adriatic front across Italy's mountainous spine in complete secrecy. An elaborate deception took place to convince the Germans of an Allied landing on Italy's west coast. Unable to locate the Canadians and convinced they must be approaching the coast, German commander Kesselring kept the Gustav Line thinly manned while spreading his sparse reserves along the coastline.[44] Meanwhile, under cover of darkness, a powerful array of Allied forces assembled near the mouth of the Liri Valley. British, French, Indian, and Canadian divisions breached the Gustav Line on May 16, forcing a German withdrawal from Cassino. The Canadian Corps took over the southern half of the Liri Valley and, together with the British XIII Corps, advanced to the next roadblock on the way to Rome.

With the collapse of the Gustav Line, the Germans withdrew sixteen kilometres to the Hitler Line, a fortification eight hundred metres deep, with weapon pits for machine guns, concrete shelters, portable steel pillboxes, and observation posts. An anti-tank ditch covered most of the front, along with barbed-wire entanglements, tripwires, and mines of ingenious design. Yet, for all their elaborate design, the German defences could not hold against the determined Allied force. The Canadians fought hard through to Pontecorvo, and on May 23, they breached the Hitler Line and pushed on to secure a bridgehead across the Melfa River.

The British Eighth Army now advanced steadily though the Liri

Valley, while the American Fifth Army at last broke free of the Anzio beachhead and captured Cisterna. Five months late, the Americans crossed the Alban Hills on their way to Rome. The 1st Canadian Corps and the rest of the Eighth Army, however, did not take part in the capture of Rome, which fell to the Americans on June 4, 1944. The Americans enjoyed their triumph for a single day — on June 6, the world's attention became riveted by D-Day on the Normandy coast, and Italy was forgotten. The capture of Rome was, in any case, a hollow victory, for in their rush to be first, the Americans failed to trap the Germans, who escaped through the mountains and reorganized their defences.[45]

The Canadians, meanwhile, were ordered to stop at Anagni, seventy-three kilometres east of Rome, and with the Liri Valley campaign at an end, they went into reserve in the Volturno Valley for two months of rest. The campaign had been costly. Between May 14 and June 4, the 1st Canadian Corps lost 789 men killed, 2,463 wounded, and 116 taken prisoner.[46] On July 31, the Canadians were visited by King George VI in the guise of "General Collingwood." He presented the Victoria Cross to Major John Mahoney of the Westminster Regiment and reviewed the Royal 22e Régiment, of which he was colonel-in-chief.

Getting to the Cemeteries and Memorials

Rome War Cemetery (pp. 78-79) is located within the ancient Aurelian city wall of Rome, adjacent to the famous Protestant Cemetery. Of the 422 Commonwealth burials here, 22 are Canadian. Due to a significant problem of theft and vandalism, the cemetery is kept locked outside the gardeners' hours. The combination for the padlock is 1221, and the padlock is at the rear of the gate, behind the two handles.[47]

By public transit: Take the Rome Metro (MEB Roma) toward Laurentina. Get off at the Piramide Metro station and walk in a westerly direction along Via del Campo Boano past the Protestant Cemetery to Via Nicola Zabaglia. Rome War Cemetery is on the left.

By car: From the Piazza del Colosseo, head west on Via Cielo Vibenna to Via San Grigorio. Continue straight onto Piazza di Porta Capena to Viale Aventino, then Piazza Albania. A short distance farther on, make a slight right at a three-branch fork onto Viale Manlio Gelsomini, which becomes Via Luigi Galvani. Turn left onto Via Nicola Zabaglia. Rome War Cemetery is 250 metres on the right.

Cassino War Cemetery and **Cassino Memorial** (p. 80) are at Cassino, 136 kilometres south of Rome. The Cassino monastery has been rebuilt and today still crowns the mountaintop. The graves in the cemetery are arranged in squares of neat rows that surround the Memorial and the Cross of Sacrifice, which overlook a reflecting pool set in a border of inlaid marble. The Memorial commemorates 4,048 Commonwealth soldiers, including 193 Canadians with no known grave. There are 4,271 Commonwealth burials in the cemetery, 289 of them unidentified. Canadian burials number 852. Unfortunately there is a serious problem of theft and vandalism to the Cemetery Register and Visitors Book, which are accessible only during the hours when the gardeners are present.

By car: From Rome's ring road, A90, exit onto A24 eastbound. Continue on A24 for about eighteen kilometres to the E45/A1 exit toward E35/ Firenze/Napoli, a toll road. Merge onto the motorway A1/E45 and travel one hundred kilometres southbound to the exit for Cassino. Exit to Cassino and, at the roundabout, take the third exit onto SR630. Go through one roundabout and take the exit toward Roma/Cassino Sud. Continue to the next roundabout and take the fourth exit onto Via Ausonia. Turn right toward SP76, then right onto SP76. Cassino War Cemetery and the Cassino Memorial are 360 metres on the right.

Minturno War Cemetery, seventy-eight kilometres north of Naples, is easily reached from Cassino or by the A1 motorway if you are coming directly from Rome. Of the 1,954 Commonwealth burials here, 32 are Canadian. The entrance to the cemetery is marked by two pillars topped by a lion on the left and an eagle on the right.

By car: From the Cassino War Cemetery, return along the SR 630 for 19.5 kilometres, crossing the A1 and going through two roundabouts. Take the exit toward Castelforte/Ss. Cosma e Damiano and merge onto SS229. Continue for four kilometres onto SP128. After another four kilometres, at the roundabout take the first exit, continue for 1.2 kilometres, then turn left toward SS7. Keep left at the fork, follow the signs for Mondragone, and merge onto SS7/Appia Road. Minturno War Cemetery is on the left.

FIGHTING IN A MUSEUM
The Bridges of Florence, June-August 1944

> [German Field Marshal Albert] Kesselring commented in 1944 that waging war in Italy was like fighting in a museum. Virtually every city, town, and village contained treasures of historical and religious significance: "frescoes, statues, churches, medieval monasteries, Roman bridges and aqueducts, Baroque fountains and Renaissance paintings." [48]

After the fall of Rome, the Eighth Army's advance toward Florence and the River Arno stalled for two weeks at the Arezzo Line, where the Germans under General Kesselring decided to make a stand. Canadian armour served in support, but their Sherman tanks ran into difficulty as they tried to advance through vineyards and fields of maize that concealed German panzers. A New Zealand division captured Arezzo at last on

Florence, Italy. The Ponte Vecchio, built in 1345 to replace an earlier bridge destroyed in a flood of the Arno. Shops fill the length of the bridge and shopkeepers flourish as they have done since medieval times. (Janice Jackson)

July 15, and the Germans withdrew across the Arno.[49] Demolitions, obstacles, and bad weather continued to slow the advance of the Eighth Army, but after a series of battles the Allies reached Florence at the beginning of August.

Meanwhile, once again in great secrecy, the Canadian Corps was moved from the Volturno Valley to the vicinity of Florence, where priceless artefacts, monuments, and remnants of antiquity were everywhere. As Kesselring commented, fighting in Italy was like fighting in a museum.[50] Both sides exploited the accessibility of choice treasures. The Allies helped themselves to souvenirs; the Germans looted on behalf of Hitler, transporting works of art for storage in northern Italy and Austria. Both sides also made an effort to preserve artefacts. Florence was largely spared the destructive bombing and shelling inflicted elsewhere. In the interests of preservation, the Germans left intact the Ponte Vecchio, oldest of the six bridges over the River Arno, and only blew up the other five. At the southern end of the Ponte Vecchio, they dynamited several medieval buildings to discourage the Allies from attempting a crossing. Railway marshalling yards, industrial zones, and roads in the battle areas around Florence were targeted by American bombers, but the historic centre remained untouched.

Getting to the Cemeteries and Memorials

Foiano della Chiana War Cemetery (p. 117) is a battlefield cemetery located in the middle of farmland thirty kilometres south of Arezzo. Most of the soldiers buried here died in the battle at the Arezzo Line in the first weeks of July 1944. Of the 256 identified burials, 6 are Canadian.

By car: From Arezzo take the A1/E35, a toll road, southbound to the exit Monte S. Savino toward SP25, another toll road. Turn right onto SP25 and continue for about four kilometres. Turn right onto Via Cassia/SS327. Go through one roundabout and after six kilometres make a slight left at Via Arezzo. Foiano della Chiana War Cemetery is 170 metres on the left.

Florence War Cemetery (p. 116) opens on the Via Aretina and extends to the banks of the River Arno. Most of the burials are from the battle for Florence, but 83, of men killed in the Appenines in the winter of 1944-45, were moved from Arrow Route Cemetery.[51] Of the 1,632 burials, 49 are Canadian.

By car: From the A1, exit onto the Florence ring-road SP127, a toll road, to Via Goffredo della Torre, which becomes Via Marco Polo after one kilometre. After about two kilometres, turn right onto Via Gen. C.A . Dalla Chiesa/SS67, which becomes Via Aretina, and continue on SS67 through one roundabout. Florence War Cemetery is 3.2 kilometres on the right at Via Aretina 38.

By public transit: From the Florence train station, walk to Stazione Valfonda and take bus 14 toward Il Girone. Get off at Girone, and the cemetery is 240 metres to the right.

Arezzo War Cemetery.
(Commonwealth War Graves Commission)

Arezzo War Cemetery reflects the makeup of the Eighth Army in the battle for Arezzo. Sixty percent of the burials are British, thirty percent are Indian. The remainder are New Zealanders, South Africans, and twenty Canadians, only seven of whom are from the period of the advance to the Arezzo Line.

By car: From Florence, take the Naples-Milan motorway/A1, a toll road, southbound for fifty-eight kilometres to the exit for Arezzo. At the roundabout, take the second exit onto Raccordo Arezzo-Battifolle and continue for about four kilometres. Take the exit toward Ponte a Chiani/Arezzo Pescaiola and merge onto SP21. Go through one roundabout and continue onto SP69 di Valdarno. At the roundabout, take the second exit to stay on SP69. Arezzo War Cemetery is 270 metres on the left.

BREAKING THE GOTHIC LINE
August 24-September 2, 1944

After a four-day interlude in Florence, the Canadians were on the move again. This time, however, the need for secrecy was cancelled when General Alexander realized the unfeasibility of the plan to cross the mountainous region from Florence to assault the centre of the Gothic Line. Although it was the shortest route, the hazards were great, and the terrain would prevent the Eighth Army from exploiting its superiority in armour and artillery. It also had little experience of large-scale operations in mountainous territory, and the French Corps, trained and experienced in mountain warfare, was committed elsewhere.

The battle to get through the Gothic Line thus shifted to the Adriatic coast, where Alexander assigned the Canadians a six-kilometre front centred on Montemaggiore. An assault on August 25 to establish bridgeheads across the Metauro River took the enemy by surprise, and four Canadian battalions had little trouble crossing the river. Tanks followed, ready for the move over the hills to the next objective, the Arzilla River.

Sharp-eyed troops spotted Prime Minister Winston Churchill accompanied by General Sir Harold Alexander in an unescorted open vehicle watching the crossing of the Metauro. Because of the risk to the British leader, they did not stay long, but it heartened troops to know their fight in Italy was not forgotten.[52]

By August 28, the Canadians had cleared the Germans from the ridge overlooking the Arzilla and were ready to tackle the considerable fortification of the Gothic Line. The Germans had turned the valley of the Foglia into a killing ground, but the minefields had been damaged by Allied aerial attacks. Defences were strangely quiet, giving the impression of enemy unpreparedness. General Kesselring assumed the British would follow their usual ponderous practice of a pause to redeploy guns and marshal resources. Instead, contrary to German expectations, the

Infantrymen of the 48th Highlanders of Canada advancing on Point 146 during the advance on the Gothic Line near the River Foglia.

(Library and Archives Canada, PA-177533)

Canadians attacked straightaway on August 30, beginning a fierce three-day battle that opened a gap in the Gothic Line.

Having broken through, the Canadians started in pursuit of the defeated enemy, and now threatened to drive a wedge between the German Tenth Army's two best divisions, the 26th Panzer Grenadiers and the 1st Parachute Battalion. To avoid complete disaster, the Germans retreated to the Green Line, a series of improvised ridges. "Though not strong in numbers, the Canadians are very good soldiers," Heinrich von Vietinghoff, commander of the German Tenth Army, observed to Kesselring.[53] A series of hard-fought battles ensued, including the costly taking of Coriano Ridge on September 13, as the Canadians made their way toward Rimini.

Despite German delaying tactics, the Canadians reached the Rimini Line on September 21. The 48th Highlanders and Royal Canadian Regiment fought to capture Rimini, but to the chagrin of the Canadians, the honour of liberating the city went to the Greek Mountain Brigade. September 22 was the last day of action for the Canadian 1st Division, its seriously depleted force replaced by New Zealanders.

From August 25 to September 22, as they moved up the Adriatic coast, the Canadian 1st Division had sustained 2,511 casualties, including 626 killed and just over 1,000 evacuated due to illness, 390 of them later fatal. Losses were heaviest among leaders of sections, platoons, and companies, invaluable men trained and experienced on the battlefield.[54]

Getting to the Cemeteries and Memorials

Ancona War Cemetery (p. 79) is six kilometres south of Ancona, which fell to the Poles on July 18, 1944, opening the port to the Allies.[55] Here, there are 1,019 Commonwealth burials, of whom 965 are identified; 161 are Canadian.

By car: From the Piazza Camillo Benzo Cavour in the centre of Ancona, take the Via Vecchini Arturo on the east side of the piazza two blocks to the Via San Martino and turn left. Continue onto Via Isonzo for 650 metres, then turn right onto Via Rodi. After 550 metres, turn left onto Via XXV Aprile. At the roundabout, take the third exit onto Via Alessandro Bocconi, which becomes Asse Nord-Sud. After 2.5 kilometres, take the Universita' exit toward Camarano and then the first right toward Strada Passo Varano. Turn right onto Strada Passo Varano. Ancona War Cemetery is 600 metres on the right.

Cesena War Cemetery (p. 117) contains 775 Commonwealth burials; 307 are Canadian.

By car: From the Milan-Rimini toll motorway A14, take the exit Cesena toward E45, also a toll road. At the roundabout, take the second exit onto Via Cervese/SS71 Bis, and continue for about three kilometres. At the roundabout, take the third exit; the parking area for Cesena War Cemetery is at the end of the road. The cemetery is within walking distance of the centre of town.

Coriano Ridge War Cemetery, located 10 kilometres south of Rimini, is, like so many, a neat rectangle in the middle of agricultural land. There are 1,885 indentified Commonwealth burials here, 427 of them Canadian.

Coriano Ridge War
Cemetery entrance.
(Commonwealth War Graves Commission)

By car: From Piazza Guiseppe Mazzini in Rimini, turn right onto Via Circonvallazione Meridionale, then, after three hundred metres, turn right again onto Via Donato Bramante. Make a slight left to rejoin Via Circonvallazione, which becomes one way for a stretch. Continue onto Via Flaminia and go through two roundabouts. At the next roundabout, take the first exit, go through one roundabout, and at the next take the second exit onto Via Coriano. Continue onto SP31 for seven kilometres, then make a slight right toward Coriano Ridge War Cemetery.

Gradara War Cemetery is steeply terraced on the side of a deep valley through which the A14 and the railroad run. Facing opposite, the valley is overlooked by the ancient Castello di Gradara. There are 1,191 Commonwealth burials in the cemetery, including 369 Canadians.

By car: From the A14/E45 Bologna-Taranto motorway, take either the exit to Pesaro or the exit to Cattolica. Take SS16 Adriatica westbound

Gradara War Cemetery.
(Commonwealth War Graves Commission)

from Pesaro or eastbound from Cattolica to SP39. Take SP39 for one kilometre, then make a slight left to Gradara War Cemetery.

Montecchio War Cemetery (p. 116) is a battlefield cemetery established by the Canadians during the fight for the Gothic Line. Later burials were brought in from the surrounding countryside. There are 582 Commonwealth burials here, of whom 288 are Canadian.

By car: From Pesaro, take Strada di Montefeltro for six kilometres, passing through six roundabouts. Continue onto SS423 and go through two roundabouts. At the third roundabout, take the third exit onto Corso XXI Gennario; the Montecchio War Cemetery is ninety-four metres on the right.

Santerno Valley War Cemetery (p. 120) is a small terraced cemetery created by the British in late 1944. There are 287 Commonwealth burials here, of whom 10 are Canadian.

By car: From Imola, a town located between Bologna and Forli, take SP610, a road that twists for over 20 kilometres through the mountains. Continue onto SS Montanara Imolese for 1.9 kilometres, then turn right to Santerno Valley War Cemetery.

By public transit: From Imola autostazione take bus 44 toward Castel del Rio (about forty-five minutes). Change to bus 145 toward Firenzuola Via Allende (about sixteen minutes). From here it is a two-minute walk to the cemetery.

THE LOMBARD PLAIN
Ideal Tank Country

> Hitler's authority remained intact. But if they could have found an escape route by removing him or discarding him, there were now those among his closest paladins who would have followed it.[56]

Having suffered defeat after defeat, General Kesselring wanted to withdraw from Italy, but Hitler, for political and administrative reasons, refused to capitulate. Above all, he was determined to hang on to the valuable industrial and agricultural regions of Upper Italy.

The invasion of Southern France had taken place in August, and had bled off a significant proportion of the Allied troops in Italy. The Fifth and Eighth Armies, now considerably weakened for want of reinforcements, could accomplish little. Although German defeat was certain and Hitler's constant interference helped to speed the process, still there was no end in sight. By now, the Eighth Army had a new commander, Sir Richard McCreery, and an elaborate battle plan drawn up by McCreery's staff. The Canadian Corps would take over a thirteen-kilometre front on the Fiumicino River, one of three successive rivers to be crossed before reaching the Po Valley.

Through December 1944, a fight over and beyond the Naviglio Canal drove the Germans to behind the Senio River dyke. It was the last full-scale battle on the Italian front for the Canadians, in the course of which they lost 548 officers and other ranks killed, 1,796 wounded, and 212 taken prisoner. In turn they captured 1,670 Germans. They buried the dead in an improvised cemetery at Villanova before pausing to celebrate Christmas.

The End of the Campaign

> Despite the strict rules, it was remarkable what the Canadians managed to take with them. The PPCLI took the Opel staff car captured at Granarolo in January, along with an assortment of small dogs stashed in individual kit bags. New Brunswick's 8th Hussars constructed a hidden compartment in the back of a truck and smuggled out Princess Louise, a horse rescued at Coriano ridge and now serving as the regimental mascot.[57] The Calgary Regiment somehow brought out a prized possession, a battered piano. . . . A group of Fifth Division truckers tried to take [five-year-old orphan] Gino Farnetti with them.[58]

Christmas 1944 for the troops in Italy was one of the best. Although there was no fraternization, for twenty-four hours guns on both sides were stilled; soldiers could relax and celebrate. The fight resumed after Christmas, but by then winter had set in, and on December 30, General Alexander called off offensive operations. The Allied forces were too weak to fight both the Germans and the weather.

Before settling down for the winter, one last operation at Granarolo cleared pockets of enemy troops at either end of the Canadian sector. The battle went like clockwork. After five days of fighting, German resistance collapsed, despite a counterattack by a group drawn from the fanatical 16th Panzer SS Division, the first and only time the Canadians fought SS troops in Italy. This was to be the last Italian battle for the Canadians.

Northwest Europe was the decisive theatre, and the Allied forces there needed to be reinforced to ensure victory. Accordingly, the Canadians in Italy were ordered to France. In Operation Penknife, devised to hoodwink the Germans, sixty thousand Canadians and thousands of vehicles moved from widely scattered locations, including Florence, Ravenna, and Cervia, to the River Senio, then collected and funnelled through two ports en route to Northwest Europe.[59] It took a month for the Germans to realize they were no longer facing the Canadians. Indeed, maps issued from

German headquarters on March 17 showed the Canadians in reserve at Ancona.

The Italian campaign was the longest sustained offensive the Allies undertook during the war. The success of the campaign can be measured by the German decision to contest the Italian peninsula, committing to the fight twenty-six divisions that might otherwise have been used in Northwest Europe and on the Eastern Front. For the Canadians, the campaign was one of forward movement, many battles, and many casualties. Of the 92,757 Canadians who served in Italy, 5,764 were dead, 19,486 wounded, and 1,006 taken prisoner. Little is to be seen, however, of the terrible struggle that took place the length and breadth of Italy. Autostrada superhighways have been built across Canadian battlefields.[60]

Getting to the Cemeteries and Memorials

There are 517 Commonwealth burials in **Padua War Cemetery**, including 14 Canadians; 32 are unidentified.

By car: The downtown core of Padua, as with many Italian cities, is a toll zone. From Padua Cathedral (Duomo di Padova), head northwest on Via Dietro Duomo and turn left onto Via Tadi. Continue onto Ponte dei Tadi, where the toll zone ends. Once across the bridge, continue onto Via San Prosdocimo, then turn right onto Via Niccoló Orsini. At the roundabout, take the third exit; at the next roundabout, take the second exit onto Piazzale do Porta Savaronola. Continue onto Via Vincenza, which becomes CavalcaVia Chiesanouva. At the roundabout, take the second exit onto Via Chiesanuova, then turn right onto Via della Biscia. Keep right to remain on Via della Biscia; Padua War Cemetery is six hundred metres on the right. The neat rectangular cemetery, bordered by Lombardy poplars and surrounded by farm fields, is reached by a fifty-metre grassy walkway.

Milan War Cemetery.
(Commonwealth War
Graves Commission)

Most of the burials in the **Milan War Cemetery** are of airmen and prisoners of war. Of 417 Commonwealth burials, 17 are Canadians: 16 members of the RCAF and 1 member of the Canadian Intelligence Corps.

By car: From Via Renato Serra southbound, continue straight onto Piazza Carlo Stuparich to Viale Elio Enrico. Turn right onto Piazzale Lorenzo Lotto, then sharp right onto Via Diomede. At the roundabout, take the first exit onto Via Ippodromo to Via Pinerolo. Turn right onto Via Harar and go through one roundabout to Via Cascina Bellaria. Milan War Cemetery is nine hundred metres on the right. A fish-scale-patterned stone path leads from the road to the entrance.

Argenta Gap War Cemetery. Argenta is a town on the SS16, midway between Ferrara and Ravenna, with Bologna at the apex of the triangle formed by the three cities. Of the 617 indentified Commonwealth burials, 76 are Canadian. Among the British burials are 2 soldiers awarded the Victoria Cross.

By car: From SS16/Via Nazionale Ponente at Agenta, exit onto Strada Sant'Antonio and go through one roundabout. Turn right, cross the railroad tracks, then turn right again and continue for 1.2 kilometres. Turn left at a corner with a stone pillar and a wall under an iron fence. Argenta Gap War Cemetery is 260 metres on the left.

Villanova Canadian War Cemetery (p. 118) is a battlefield burial ground chosen by the 5th Canadian Armoured Division after heavy fighting at the River Lamone. Villanova is located near the centre of the triangle formed by Ravenna, Ferrara, and Bologna. The long and narrow cemetery runs along the road at the edge of the village. A small gothic-style marble building at the entrance houses the Register and Visitors Book. Of the 212 Commonwealth burials here, 205 are Canadian.

By car: From Ferrara southbound or Ravenna northbound, take SS16/ Strada Statale Adriatica to SP25 at Mezzana. Turn onto SP25, go through one roundabout, and at the next roundabout take the first exit to Via della Chiesa. From Bologna, take the A14/E45 toll road toward Ancona for thirty-four kilometres to the exit toward Ravenna. Merge onto A14 and continue for twelve kilometres to the exit for Bagnacavallo. Take the exit and continue straight to the roundabout. Take the first exit onto SP8 and continue onto SP253 for about four kilometres. Turn left onto SP25 and continue for six kilometres. Turn left onto Largo Tre Guinchi and continue onto Via della Chiesa. Villanova Canadian War Cemetery is three hundred metres on the right.

Ravenna War Cemetery is located in the countryside thirteen kilometres west of Ravenna, just off the road to Ferrara. The 100 metre grass path to the cemetery leads from a farmhouse with its surrounding outbuildings to the pillared entrance gates. Of the 955 Commonwealth burials, 436 are Canadian. "Among those buried in the cemetery are thirty-three men of the Jewish Infantry Brigade Group which was formed in September 1944, chiefly by volunteers from Palestine; the burials at Ravenna form the largest concentration of casualties from the Brigade."[61]

By car: From Ravenna, take SP1 northbound; at the roundabout, take the first exit onto Via Fossa Dimiglio. Continue onto Via Zanelli Naviglio;

at the roundabout, take the second exit onto Via G. Fuschini. At the next roundabout, take the first exit onto Via Faetina. At the next roundabout, take the first exit onto the ramp for SS16, direction Bologna/Ferrara/Venezia, and merge onto SS16/Strada Statale 16 Adriatica. Continue for five kilometres, then turn left onto SP20; the turnoff toward Ravenna War Cemetery is one kilometre on the left.

More than half the Commonwealth burials in **Staglieno Cemetery** are from World War I, when Genoa was a base for British Empire forces. Among the 122 World War II burials are 4 Canadians who served with the RCAF.

By car: From Genoa on SS45 northbound turn right onto Ponte Frederico Campanella, then take the first left onto Corso Alessandro de Stefanis and continue onto Lungobisagno Istria. Turn left onto Ponte Giulio Monteverde. The Monumental Cemetery of Staglieno is straight ahead, a large communal cemetery laid out like the nave of a church. The CWGC burial ground is three hundred metres from the entrance on a steeply terraced hillside. A sign "British Cemetery" points the direction to a stairway.

Staglieno Cemetery, Genoa. (Commonwealth War Graves Commission)

PART V

The Canadians in Northwest Europe

Overlord would be the largest amphibious operation in history, with more than 5,000 ships, 8,000 aircraft and eight divisions in the first wave. There was considerable nervousness, known as "D-Day jitters." . . . But the planning which went into Operation Neptune — the Channel crossing stage of Overlord — was extraordinary in its detail. On receiving their orders, which ran to several hundred pages, the 3rd Canadian Division dubbed it "Operation Overboard."[1]

As plans for the invasion of Europe developed, the Canadians were determined to have a presence on D-Day. With the 1st Division fighting in Italy and the 2nd Division still recovering from Dieppe, General McNaughton informed General Crerar, commander of the 1st Canadian Corps, that the 3rd Canadian Infantry Division had been selected for special training in preparation for Operation Overlord, the landing of British, Canadian, Free French, and American forces on the beaches of Normandy. The Canadian 3rd Division had been formed in the summer of 1940 in response to the emergency created by the German invasion of Norway and Denmark. Under the command of Major-General R.F.L. "Rod" Keller and the close scrutiny of Montgomery, staff officers transformed the division into a smooth-running unit ready for D-Day. With the beaches of Normandy in mind, their training focused on getting ashore and staying there.

Twenty first Army Group controlled the two field armies assigned to the Normandy operation. The formation, commanded by General Montgomery, consisted of the British Second Army and First Canadian

Army. Despite being allotted to Operation Overlord, the men did not receive the basic weaponry for the invasion until late 1943. New anti-tank guns such as the PIAT (Projector, Infantry, Anti-Tank), the 6-pounder, the 17-pounder, the M10 self-propelled, and the Sherman tank required a good deal of training, but by dint of focused preparation, the 21st Army Group was made ready for battle.[2]

The Germans in France

The enemy, too, had learned lessons from Dieppe, which affirmed Hitler's belief in the ability of the Atlantic Wall to defeat a seaborne invasion. Elaborate fortified gun positions, small concrete shelters called "Tobruks" ingeniously made from the turrets of disabled tanks, and eight thousand units of a planned fifteen thousand permanent fortifications had been completed by July 1943.

On Hitler's orders, most of the work had been concentrated in the Pas de Calais, across the strait from Dover, the closest crossing to France from England. In fact, few German senior officers believed in an invasion of a peninsula so far from the German border that it could be easily sealed off. To them, the twenty-nine kilometres of Normandy coast between the River Orne and the cliffs at Arromanches-les-Bains seemed a more likely possibility, and they quietly saw to the construction of two strongpoints at Franceville and Riva Bella. Resistance nests, built around gun casements, were sited along the dunes, but the six-foot-thick walls of concrete around the guns meant they could only fire along the beach in enfilade, leaving flanks and rear vulnerable.

Owing to the need at the Russian and Italian fronts for so many soldiers, the Germans were experiencing a shortage of manpower. As well, the construction of defences tied down great numbers of troops, but the German belief that a strong fortress required fewer troops made the shortage acceptable.[3] The best personnel had been taken as reinforcements for the war on the Russian front, leaving static coastal divisions made up of eighteen-year-olds, men over thirty-five, men recovering from third-

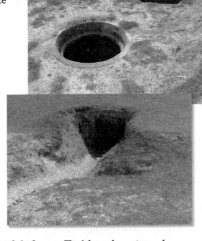

Right: German-made "Tobruks," small concrete shelters made from the turrets of disabled tanks. These are found in the sand dunes at Courseulles-sur-Mer, Normandy. (Susan Evans Shaw)

Below right: Courseulles-sur-Mer, Normandy. Entrance to an underground installation. (Susan Evans Shaw)

degree frostbite, and reluctant Red Army prisoners.[4]

Front-line defences of pillboxes, concrete bunkers, and underground installations lined the beaches, but without a continuous secondary line of defence. Field and anti-tank guns were dug in three to six kilometres behind the coast, and reserve companies were quartered inland to contain invading Allied troops that might break away from the beaches. In March 1944, the arrival of the top-class 352nd Mobile Infantry strengthened defences, as did a move in May of the 21st Panzer Division to Caen. Meanwhile Field Marshal Erwin Rommel, commanding the German forces along the French coast, initiated mine laying and construction of deadly beach obstacles.

> If Hitler and his generals could agree on a coherent reaction to an invasion, Operation Overlord might prove to be a costly enterprise.[5]

Fortunately for the Allied invasion, Hitler refused a unified command in France so that he could maintain control by his policy of divide and rule. With the power concentrated in his own hands, he denied his commanders the power they needed to win his battles. This state of affairs left Field Marshal Gerd von Rundstedt, commander-in-chief of the western sector, with no option but to prepare against invasion with limited and inadequate authority. Rommel became increasingly convinced the attack would be in the Normandy sector. Hitler vacillated, but, on balance, was inclined to favour the Pas de Calais.[6]

The Plan of Attack

The Allies had to do what no-one had done since William the Conqueror, and that Philip of Spain, Louis XIV, Napoleon and Hitler had all attempted in vain. In two days they had to transport across the stormy tidal waters of the Channel, without hurt from U-boat, mine, E-boat or Luftwaffe nearly 200,000 armed men and land them with 20,000 mechanical vehicles on open beaches.[7]

The sector of coast chosen for Overlord stretched between the Orne and the Vire river estuaries on the Normandy coast and along the eastern shore of the Cherbourg Peninsula of Brittany. Beaches here were mostly sheltered from the prevailing westerly winds and within range of fighter aircraft based in England. On the right (eastern) flank would be the US First Army under Lieutenant-General Omar Bradley, and on the left (western) flank, the British Second Army under Lieutenant-General Sir Miles Dempsey. Bradley's Americans were to land at beaches designated Omaha and Utah and capture bridgeheads between the Drôme and Vire Rivers and the eastern shore of the peninsula. Dempsey was to seize Port-en Bessin, Bayeux, Cabourg at the mouth of the Dives, and the communications centre of Caen. The British forces would land at Gold and Sword Beaches, with the Canadians sandwiched in the middle, landing at Juno Beach.[8] The Canadian component comprised three divisions of an armoured brigade, a parachute battalion, and No. 2 Army Group Royal Canadian Artillery. Unlike at Dieppe, there were no cliff-top positions overlooking Juno. The landing terrain was better, and the troops would be covered by firepower from the RAF and the US Army Air Force. The navy would provide battleships, cruisers, and a host of small support vessels.

Various factors were needed to contribute to the success of Overlord. The Soviets would have to continue to engage the energies of two-thirds of the German Army. Designed to deceive the enemy that the invasion would take place at the Pas de Calais, an elaborate deception, codenamed Fortitude, would keep German troops busy and away from Normandy with preparations to defend the coast of Calais. From April 24, the First Canadian Army participated in Operation Quicksilver, which disseminated fictional messages by wireless to build up a picture of the army preparing to attack the Pas de Calais.

Initial plans for the campaign called for the attack to proceed in a series of managed phases. Invading troops, once ashore, would establish and defend a bridgehead to include Caen, the centre of the rail and road network in Normandy and vital for the establishment of air fields. The Americans would capture Cherbourg and Brest, and establish a new port at Quiberon Bay. If nothing else, their activity would focus attention on Brittany. Once established on the beaches, troops would move inland as swiftly as possible. At all costs, there must be no repetition of the slaughter at Dieppe. Shelling of targets had to be accurate and on time. Victory was planned at a blood price the Allies could afford.[9]

> Today is D-Day . . . London is very quiet — D-Day is being taken as another in the normal course of events. It never enters anyone's mind here that our lads won't keep on going until they reach Berlin. They may have setbacks but they'll get there.[10]

The Landings in Normandy, June 6, 1944

> The defeat and near destruction of two German armies in just seventy-six days was one of the most remarkable military victories of the Second World War. It was a victory won primarily by Allied soldiers employing flexible and innovative operational and tactical solutions to the challenges confronting them. The Canadians

played a role in this victory all out of proportion to the number of troops engaged. Their performance at both the tactical and operational level was far from perfect but it compares favourably with that of any other army in Normandy.[11]

The British and Canadians sailed from Portsmouth, while the Americans sailed from ports farther west. All arrived at the assembly area known as Zone "Z," southeast of the Isle of Wight. A barrier of German mines lay interposed between the approaching Allied ships and the Normandy beaches, so British and Canadian minesweepers were tasked with breaching the barrier to prepare channels for passage. As the minesweepers approached the French coast, there was a risk they would be spotted, warning the German defenders an attack was under way. But the German shore batteries did not fire on the sweepers, which proceeded to clear ten channels marked with lighted buoys. Two miniature British submarines, in position close to shore, guided landing craft as they closed on the beaches. Unfortunately, the weather was too rough to permit the launch of dinghies to mark the separate points where DD (Duplex Drive) amphibious tanks were to be launched by the 8th Canadian Infantry Brigade. Headquarters ship HMS *Hilary* served the 3rd Canadian Division off the coast of Normandy as it had served the 1st Canadian Division the same capacity in the assault on Sicily.[12]

Bernières-sur-Mer (Juno Beach) house liberated by the Queen's Own Rifles of Canada and seen in the original 1944 film of the D-Day landing. (Susan Evans Shaw)

The first Canadians to land in Normandy were dropped by Horsa glider. Those who landed near the objective secured the drop zone near Varaville. (Susan Evans Shaw)

RAF Bomber Command began its attack upon ten selected coastal batteries at thirty minutes before midnight on June 5, 1944. No German soldiers died in the attack and damage was minimal, but the bombing succeeded in disorganizing and demoralizing the defenders. Then, shortly after midnight, British and American airborne divisions began landing in drop zones behind the beaches. Gliders landed elements of the Oxfordshire and Buckinghamshire Light Infantry and a party of engineers, which captured Pegasus Bridge over the Canal de Caen à la Mer near Bernouville and the nearby Ranville Bridge over the Orne River.

The first Canadians to land in Normandy were members of "C" Company, 1st Canadian Parachute Battalion. Darkness and boggy ground interfered with parachute drops, and the battalion was scattered far from the drop zone. Eighty-four men landed in enemy hands and were taken prisoner. The fragmented battalion nevertheless succeeded in carrying out a plan to destroy certain bridges while others seized and held ground objectives.[13] Those who did land near the objective took the Germans by surprise. Unopposed, they secured the drop zone near Varaville.[14]

Meanwhile, a rough Channel with waves five to six feet high made conditions terrible for the approaching landing craft. Most of the soldiers and some sailors were miserably seasick. The rough sea also spoiled the

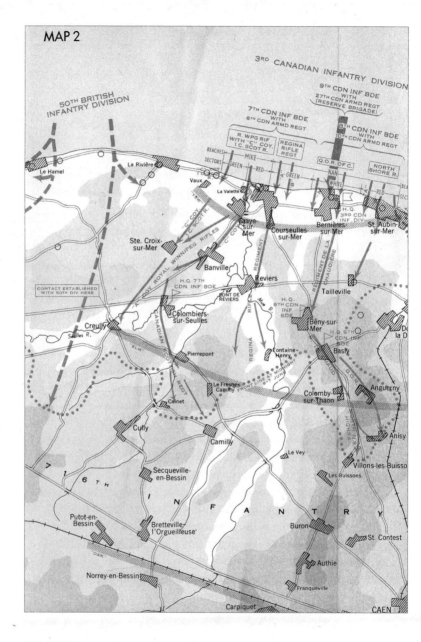

MAP 2

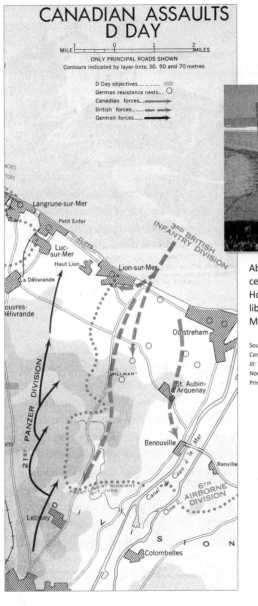

CANADIAN ASSAULTS
D DAY

MILE |———|———| 0 |———|———| 1 |———|———| 2 MILES

ONLY PRINCIPAL ROADS SHOWN
Contours indicated by layer-tints: 30, 50 and 70 metres

D Day objectives..........
German resistance nests... ○
Canadian forces.._____→
British forces......_ _ _ →
German forces...._____▶

Langrune-sur-Mer
Petit Enfer
Luc-sur-Mer
CLIFFS
Haut Lion
La Délivrande
Lion-sur-Mer
3RD BRITISH INFANTRY DIVISION
ouvres-Délivrande
Ouistreham
21ST PANZER DIVISION
"HILLMAN"
St. Aubin-d'Arquenay
Benouville
Ranville
Canal de Caen à la Mer
Orne R. à la Mer
6TH AIRBORNE DIVISION
FRONT LINE AT MIDNIGHT 6-7 JUNE
D I V I S I O N
Lebisey
Colombelles

Above: Stele plaque celebrating the Fort Garry Horse and their part in the liberation of Bernières-sur-Mer, Normandy. (Susan Evans Shaw)

Source: C.P. Stacey, *Official History of the Canadian Army in the Second World War. Volume III: The Victory Campaign: The Operations in North-West Europe, 1944-1945* (Ottawa: Queen's Printer, 1966), map 2.

Left: Churchill tank "Charlie." Graye-sur-Mer, Normandy.
(Susan Evans Shaw)

Below left: Graye-sur-Mer landing place of Canadians.
(Susan Evans Shaw)

planned neat pattern of the landings. Surprisingly, enemy air and ground forces took no action against the approaching flotilla, and only after men and assault craft touched shore did fierce opposition begin. As the assault craft moved toward the beaches, naval destroyers and landing craft guns fired on enemy strongpoints, destroying buildings but doing little damage to the concrete defences. Seven of the Canadians' DD tanks were lost, but thanks to the rubber dinghies they carried, most of the crews were rescued. Those tanks that did make it to shore stopped on the seaward side of the beach obstacles, and fired on the nearest pillboxes.

Despite the formidable defences, the assaulting Canadians managed to breach the seawall, infiltrating the German defences and attacking from the rear. Beach obstacles, booby-trapped houses, sniper fire, and defensive fire all took their toll. Seaborne Canadian losses on June 6 amounted to 340 all ranks killed or died of wounds, 574 wounded, and 47 taken prisoner. All in all, the D-Day achievement was magnificent: for a total of 10,000 Allied combatants dead, wounded, and taken prisoner, far fewer than had been feared, the Atlantic Wall had been breached and the way opened for a victorious campaign. For Canada, the day was notable inasmuch as all three Canadian services—army, navy, and air force—had fought together.

Above: Juno Beach Centre western aspect. (Janice Jackson)

Below: Present-day Juno Beach, Normandy. (Janice Jackson)

Top: Varaville Château Gatehouse. Six men of the 1st Canadian Parachute Battalion were killed in this gatehouse on June 6, 1944, by an enemy shell fired from a German bunker within sight of the second-floor window.
(Susan Evans Shaw)

Above: Plaque at Varaville Memorial, Normandy dedicated to the six men. "The Canadians as part of the 6th British Airborne Division continued their attack until the German troops in the bunker surrendered."
(Susan Evans Shaw)

Liberation monument on the D-Day beach at Bernières-sur-Mer, Normandy. (Susan Evans Shaw)

Bény-sur-Mer Canadian War Cemetery, Reviers, Normandy, France.
(Susan Evans Shaw)

Ryes War Cemetery.
(Commonwealth War Graves Commission)

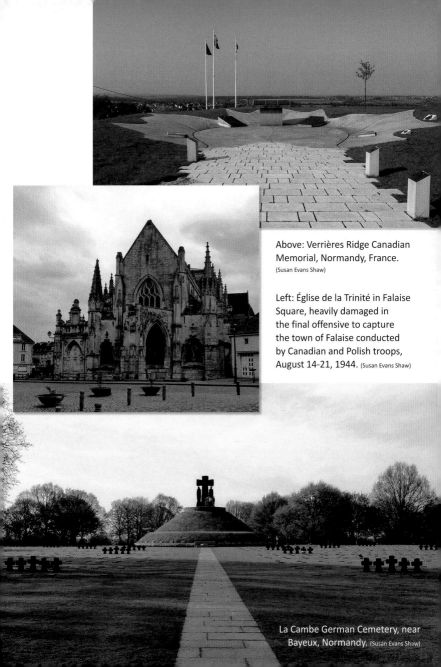

Above: Verrières Ridge Canadian Memorial, Normandy, France. (Susan Evans Shaw)

Left: Église de la Trinité in Falaise Square, heavily damaged in the final offensive to capture the town of Falaise conducted by Canadian and Polish troops, August 14-21, 1944. (Susan Evans Shaw)

La Cambe German Cemetery, near Bayeux, Normandy. (Susan Evans Shaw)

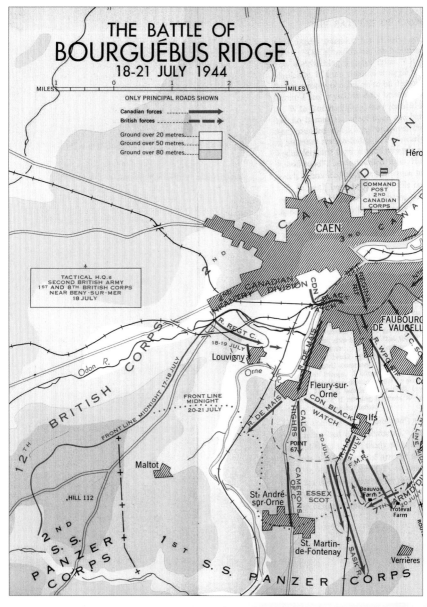

THE BATTLE OF
BOURGUÉBUS RIDGE
18-21 JULY 1944

MILES 1   0   1   2   3 MILES

ONLY PRINCIPAL ROADS SHOWN

Canadian forces --------->
British forces --------->

Ground over 20 metres......
Ground over 50 metres......
Ground over 80 metres......

Héro

COMMAND
POST
2ND
CANADIAN
CORPS

CAEN

TACTICAL H.Q.s
SECOND BRITISH ARMY
1ST AND 8TH BRITISH CORPS
NEAR BENY-SUR-MER
18 JULY

CANADIAN DIVISION

FAUBOURG
DE VAUCELL

R. REGT C.

Odon R.

BRITISH CORPS

18-19 JULY

Louvigny

Orne

FRONT LINE MIDNIGHT 17-18 JULY

FRONT LINE
MIDNIGHT
20-21 JULY

R. DE MAIS

CALG HIGHRS

CAMERONS OF C

Fleury-sur-Orne

CDN BLACK

WATCH

Ifs

POINT
67

20 JULY

F.M.R.

21 JULY

Maltot

Beauvoir
Farm

7TH ARMD DIV

30 JULY

Troteval
Farm

.HILL 112

2ND
S.S.
PANZER
CORPS

1ST

St. André-
sur-Orne

ESSEX
SCOT

St. Martin-
de-Fontenay

R. SASK R.

Verrières

S.S. PANZER CORPS

Source: C.P. Stacey, *Official History of the Canadian Army in the Second World War.*
Volume III: The Victory Campaign: The Operations in North-West Europe, 1944-1945
(Ottawa: Queen's Printer, 1966), map 3.

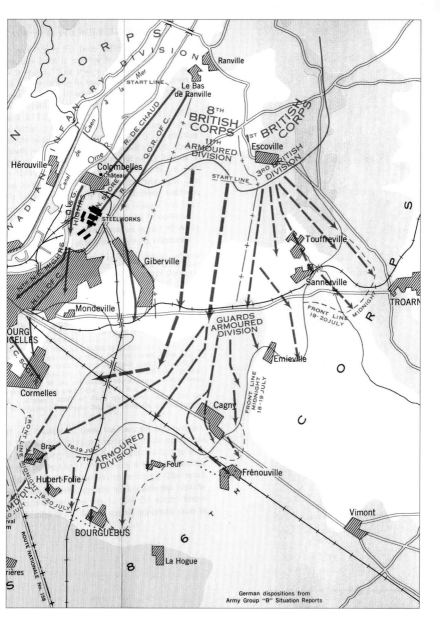

German dispositions from
Army Group "B" Situation Reports

Above and left:
Bretteville-sur-Laize Canadian
War Cemetery entrance.
Normandy, France.

(Susan Evans Shaw)

Right: Place Gérard Doré outside the
entrance to Bretteville-sur-Laize Canadian
War Cemetery memorial and plaque
for Private Gérard Doré, who joined the
Fusiliers de Mont-Royal Battalion, age 15,
killed in action at Verrières on
July 23, 1944, age 16. (Susan Evans Shaw)

Getting to the Cemeteries and Memorials

Pegasus Memorial 2nd Horsa Glider

By car: From the Caen ring road N814/E46, take the exit for D515 eastbound toward Bénouville/Merville-Franceville/Cabourg/Port de Plaisance/De Ouistreham. Merge onto D 515 and continue for 7.6 kilometres. Take the D514 exit to Bénouville and continue straight for about five hundred metres. At the roundabout, take the second exit onto avenue du Commandant Kieffer/D514. Cross the canal on the new Pegasus Bridge and turn left onto Impasse Pegasus. The turn is well signed, and the Pegasus Memorial building is on the right. The outdoor display includes a Horsa glider that carried parachutists to their drop zone.

Top: Pegasus Bridge Museum, Ranville, Normandy.
(Susan Evans Shaw)

Left: The original bridge, nicknamed Pegasus after the shoulder emblem worn by the British airborne forces, now in the grounds of the Varaville Museum. (Susan Evans Shaw)

Ranville War Cemetery contains 2,235 Commonwealth burials of World War II, 78 of which are Canadian. There are also 330 German graves, 97 unidentified, and a few burials of other nationalities.

By car: From the Pegasus Memorial return to D514. At the second roundabout take the second exit onto D37 and continue for 1.2 kilometres. Turn sharp left onto rue Airbornes 10. Ranville War Cemetery is at the end of the road and on the left behind the community cemetery.

Varaville Memorial (p. 154). Six men of the 1st Canadian Parachute Battalion were killed in the Varaville Château Gatehouse on June 6, 1944, by an enemy shell fired from a German bunker within sight of the second-floor window.

By car: From Ranville War Cemetery, return along rue Airbornes 10 to D37, make a slight right and continue for 2.2 kilometres to D513 and turn left. Follow D513 for 5.8 kilometres to the intersection with D95 (Route de Varaville). The monument to the Canadian parachutists stands at the apex of the intersection, a Canadian flag clearly visible.

Bayeux War Cemetery contains 4,144 burials, of which 178 are Canadian and 338 are unidentified. Other nationalities, mainly German, number 505.

By car: From Caen take the N13 for just over 25 kilometres to exit 37.1 toward Le Molay-Littry. Turn right onto D5/Route de Littry and continue for 1.6 kilometres, then turn right to remain on D5. The Bayeux Cemetery is 200 metres on the right. The **Bayeux Memorial** is on the left side of the road opposite the cemetery. Names on the Memorial are those of more than 1,800 Commonwealth soldiers who died in the early weeks

after the Normandy landing and have no known grave. Of these, 338 are Canadian.

Beny-sur-Mer Canadian War Cemetery

(p. 156) contains mainly men of the Third Canadian Division who died on June 6, 1944, and the following days during the advance toward Caen. Of the 2,029 identified burials, 2,025 are Canadian. Nineteen burials are unidentified.

By car: On Caen's peripheral road, N814, head northeast to exit 5-Côte de Nacre toward Douvres-la-Déliverande/Courseulles-sur-Mer. At the roundabout, take the third exit onto avenue de la Côte de Nacre. After 1.4 kilometres, go through one roundabout and keep right to stay on avenue de la Côte de Nacre. Continue onto D7. Pass through one roundabout and at the next take the fourth exit to D404 and continue for 5.5 kilometres. At the roundabout, take the third exit onto D35 toward Reviers. The cemetery is just over 1 kilometre on the right.

Reviers, Normandy, Grave of Private Rudolph Albert Cochius, killed June 6, 1944, age 20. Beny-sur-Mer Canadian War Cemetery. (Susan Evans Shaw)

There are 652 Commonwealth burials in the **Ryes War Cemetery** (p. 156), of whom 21 are Canadian. There are also 1 Polish and 352 German burials.

By car: Travelling northwest on Bayeux's peripheral road, N613, exit onto D12/Route de Courseulles toward Ver-sur-Mer. After three kilometres turn left onto D205, then continue on D112 for 2.4 kilometres. Turn right onto D87. The cemetery is 300 metres on the left.

The **Juno Beach Centre** (p. 153), located at Courseulles-sur-Mer opened June 6, 2003. The Centre presents the war effort made by all Canadians, civilian and military alike, both at home and on the various fronts during the Second World War.

By car: In courseulles-sur-Mer take D514 (rue de la Mer) which becomes rue Maréchal Foch after a left turn. Continue on D514 for 700 metres then make a right turn onto rue de Marine Dunkerque. After 250 metres turn right onto voie des Français Libres. The Juno Beach Centre is 230 metres on the left.

The Bridgehead Battle, June 7-30, 1944

The Allied invasion of June 6 took the German force in Normandy by surprise. Hitler remained convinced that the landings there were only a sideshow and that the main effort would be an assault at the Pas de Calais. As insurance, he kept the entire Fifteenth Army at Calais, where it waited for an attack that never came.[15]

At dawn on June 7, troops of the 7th (Royal Winnipeg Rifles, Regina Rifle Regiment, and 1st Battalion The Canadian Scottish Regiment) and 9th (Highland Light Infantry of Canada, Stormont, Dundas and

Glengarry Highlanders, and North Nova Scotia Highlanders) Canadian Brigades, supported by the 9th British Brigade, resumed their drive toward Carpiquet and Caen. The advance did not go smoothly. The British brigade, on the Canadian left, encountered sharp resistance from the 21st Panzer Division, and by mid afternoon had only reached Cambes-en-Plaine, five kilometres northwest of Caen. The 9th Canadian Brigade carried on toward Carpiquet with an unprotected left flank. For them it was vital to get inland, stake out ground, and take possession of the airport at Carpiquet.

Colonel Kurt Meyer, commander of the 12th Panzer Division, watched the approach of the Canadians from his eyrie in the tower of the church at Abbaye d'Ardennes. Anticipating their objective at Authie, he ordered his troops to attack and take the village.[16] The 9th Canadian Brigade fell back on Buron, where an even longer and bloodier battle ensued until the Canadians were driven back to Villons-les-Buissons, about five kilometres northwest of Caen. Here they dug in and held on for the next month while Caen remained in German hands.[17] Canadian losses that day were greater than those any Anglo-Canadian unit had suffered on D-Day: 110 killed, 64 wounded, and 128 taken prisoner.

Elements of the German 21st Panzers and the 716th Division held well-camouflaged positions along the road to Carpiquet, but after a series of time-consuming engagements through to the first week of July, the North Nova Scotias and the 2nd Canadian Armoured Brigade managed to clear the village of Buron and press forward to Authie, the last outpost before Carpiquet. Here, the 12th SS Panzer Division *Hitlerjugend* (Hitler Youth), commanded by Colonel Meyer, came into action. The outnumbered platoons of North Nova Scotias and Cameron Highlanders of Ottawa put up a good fight but were eventually overcome. While the battle raged, the fanatical Hitler Youth began murdering Canadian prisoners. In the courtyard of the Abbaye d'Ardenne, below Meyer's observation tower, eighteen North Nova Scotia Highlanders and Sherbrooke Fusiliers of the 2nd Armoured Brigade were executed in cold blood.[18]

Meanwhile, to the south of Authie, the 7th Canadian Brigade and the 6th Canadian Armoured Regiment had dug in at Putot-en-Bessin, with anti-tank guns positioned at the ready. Defence of the town came at a heavy cost in casualties and men taken prisoner, but it prevented the Germans from advancing to the Caen-Bayeux highway and kept them from the beaches at Courseulles. In retaliation, the fanatical youngsters of the 12th SS Panzers summarily executed twenty-six more Canadian POWs, members of the Royal Winnipeg Rifles and the 6th Armoured Regiment held at Château d'Audrieu.

An operation involving units that had never worked or trained together is asking for trouble. Ordered to attack through Norrey-en-Bessin to Le Mesnil-Patry and seize the high ground three kilometres south of Cheux, units of the 69th British Brigade, the 6th Canadian Armoured Brigade, and the Queen's Own Rifles could not coordinate their movements. In consequence, they ran straight into an SS Panzer Grenadier ambush and suffered terrible losses.[19]

Despite these setbacks, the Allied forces were now firmly established on the Continent. Over 300,000 men, 54,000 vehicles, and 106,000 metric tonnes of stores made for a considerable presence, as did the British and Canadian formations now linked up with the Americans to form a continuous line all along the front. The great armoured counteroffensive planned by the Germans to drive the invaders back into the sea had failed.[20]

Beny-sur-Mer Canadian War Cemetery, Normandy. Grave of Sergeant Frederick Bernard Harris, Queen's Own Rifles, killed June 7, 1944. (Susan Evans Shaw)

The Battles of Caen and Bourguébus, July 1-23, 1944

> "The Commander [Crerar] has certain qualities which are assets,"
> Monty acknowledged. "But taken all round I consider he is not
> good enough to command a Canadian division; the Canadian
> soldier is such a magnificent chap that he deserves, and should
> be given, really good generals."[21]

Montgomery now turned his attention on the capture of Caen, which,
along with Carpiquet, had airfields that were badly needed to reduce
RAF casualties and loss of planes over the Channel. Operation Epsom
went into play on June 25 and lasted a week. Enemy resistance was
intense owing to the fanatical 12th SS Panzer Division *Hitlerjugend*,
which fought with formidable determination. Casualties on both sides
were considerable. Montgomery called off Epsom and the capture of
Caen, to the fury of the already frustrated RAF officials.

Meanwhile, Rommel took charge of the German forces and ordered
a move to defensive warfare. He planned to contain the Allies between
the coast and the flooded Dives River valley. A
month of static warfare followed, with conditions somewhat like those of the Western Front
in World War I, with soldiers on both sides living
in slit trenches or bunkers. To add to the general
discomfort, rain fell non-stop and prolonged the
mosquito season. The next operation went in on

Caen after its capture. "Although William the
Conqueror's Two Great Abbeys Still Stood Up
Proud and Austere, Whole Quarters of the Place
Had Been Reduced to Rubble."

(Source: C.P. Stacey, *Official History of the Canadian Army in the Second World
War. Volume III: The Victory Campaign: The Operations in North-West Europe,
1944-1945* (Ottawa: Queen's Printer, 1966), 81

July 4. Designed to capture Carpiquet airfield and eliminate an observation post in the village, the 8th Canadian Brigade (Queen's Own Rifles of Canada, Le Régiment de la Chaudière, and the North Shore [New Brunswick] Regiment) succeeded in taking the village of Carpiquet and the airfield's northern hangars, but the Royal Winnipeg Rifles were not so successful. Heavy resistance from the 12th SS Panzers, holed up in pillboxes outside the southern hangars and control buildings, forced the Winnipeggers to retreat, leaving the airfield in enemy hands.[22] The partial victory cost the 8th Brigade and the Rifles a total of 377 casualties, including 127 dead.

Lieutenant-General John Crocker, commander of the 1st British Corps, which included the 3rd Canadian Division, blamed the unsatisfactory outcome on the Canadian leadership and divisional commander, Major-General Rod Keller. His complaint reached Montgomery, who, for his part, was not happy with First Canadian Army commander Harry Crerar and his lack of battlefield experience. Montgomery made no changes, but the situation strained relations between the Canadian and British commands.

The move toward Caen, the next objective, opened with an attack by Halifax and Lancaster bombers, which levelled northern sectors of the city. Every available troop, weapon, and heavy artillery was brought to bear on the assault. The Canadian 9th Brigade again confronted the tenacious 12th SS Panzer Division *Hitlerjugend*, but eventually overpowered their defences. On the evening of July 8, Rommel ordered a withdrawal from the city, but continued to hold the high ground west and south of Caen. Allied divisions paid a heavy price for their capture of Caen — three thousand killed, wounded, or missing — but the bridgehead the Allies established forced the Germans to bring in their local reserve to extend the length of their defence line. Without reserves, the Germans could no longer plan on concentrating against the Americans.[23]

Allied command, however, had no idea how close the enemy was to collapse. The Germans were suffering a growing loss of confidence in their cause, their leaders, and their *Führer*. Allied leaders, distracted by worry over manpower shortages, failed to pick up on intelligence relating to the enemy's state of mind. Instead of continuing an offensive that could have brought the Germans to their knees, they retired to await reinforcements.[24] The timely arrival of the 2nd Canadian Division from England, along with the 2nd Canadian Group Royal Artillery, relieved worries over a manpower shortage, but the newly arrived force was a mix of veterans and green troops. While the next operation was being planned, Major-General Guy Simonds ordered the inexperienced recruits forward to accustom them to the feeling of being under fire.

The next order of business was to dislodge the Germans from their position south of Caen, where they occupied the high ground at Bourguébus and Verrières. In turn, this action would lend support to Operation Cobra, the US First Army's advance to St-Lô, west of the Orne River. RAF Bomber Command and the US 8th Air Force opened the assault by bombing enemy positions in the areas of the Allied advance.[25] Simonds concentrated on Verrières Ridge, a kidney-shaped height of land rising to eighty-eight metres above the plain, not unlike Vimy Ridge. In fact, Simonds was anxious to prove that he and his corps were worthy successors to Arthur Currie and the Canadian Corps of 1917. Unlike the British command, held somewhat in check by haunting memories of the Somme bloodbath, the Canadians thought in terms of bold, successful attacks in the style of Vimy.[26] But despite dogged assaults by three strong Canadian regiments—Les Fusiliers Mont-Royal, the Essex Scottish, and the South Saskatchewans—Verrières Ridge remained in enemy hands.

The attempt on the two ridges at Bourguébus and Verrières came to an end on July 22. Casualties of 6,168 men killed, wounded, and missing amounted to a human cost that seriously reduced the combat power of the Anglo-Canadian armies. On the enemy side, the battle for the ridges contributed to the Germans' eventual defeat—as their casualties mounted, they had to bring in scarce reserves to replace the losses.

The Breakout Begins, July 24-31, 1944

> Generations of young Americans would be brought up to believe
> . . . that victory in Normandy had been achieved by American
> guts and genius while the British "sat on their butts." . . . No
> good therefore would be served by reminding Americans that
> their stunning successes in France in 1944 were predicated on
> the selfless role of British and Canadian troops . . . the battle for
> Normandy was the greatest, the most decisive and the most Allied
> in its conception and relentless, painstaking execution.[27]

Operation Spring, a second attack on Verrières Ridge, took place on July 25. In an assault led by Major F. Philip Griffin, the Black Watch Regiment made it to the flat top of the ridge but ran straight into a well-camouflaged enemy position backed by tanks. Not more than fifteen men made it back to their own lines. The body of Major Griffin was later found among the many dead on the top of the ridge.[28] Operation Spring ended as the bloodiest single day for Canadian arms except for

Dieppe,[29] and resulted in the near-extinction of the Black Watch Regiment. Altogether, the corps suffered 1,500 casualties, 405 of them fatal.

The lone success of Spring went to the Royal Hamilton Light Infantry, the "Rileys." Their commander, Dieppe survivor Lieutenant-Colonel Denis Whitaker, had been wounded earlier and Brigadier John

Bretteville-sur-Laize Canadian War Cemetery grave of Major F. Philip Griffin of the Black Watch Regiment, killed in action at Verrières Ridge. (Susan Evans Shaw)

Rockingham took command. The Rileys succeeded in taking Verrières village. The enemy could come at them only over the top of the ridge, and the silhouetted attackers made easy targets for artillery fire.[30] The Rileys and the 2nd Anti-Tank Regiment held firm in the village, and on July 26 they repelled an attack by the 9th SS Panzer Corps as it attempted to restore the former battle line.[31]

The Falaise Road: Operation Totalize, August 7-10, 1944

> Attempting to drive through from Trun to Falaise . . . I was stunned
> to see the carnage. Bloated bodies and still smouldering vehicles
> were scattered for miles along the road. I had witnessed many
> scenes of death and destruction before in Sicily and Italy, but never
> anything on a scale such as this.[32]

On August 4, Montgomery issued a new directive: the Canadians would help force the enemy back across the Seine. In an operation designated Totalize, Montgomery planned a carefully staged advance toward Falaise, attacking by night to reduce the advantage of the German long-range weaponry. Heavy bombers would neutralize enemy defences and armour.

The Canadian 2nd Division was more than a thousand men under strength, even with the addition of the Essex Scottish and the Royal Regiment of Canada. Both battalions had been reconstituted since late July, and each had been assigned a new commanding officer. During a period of rest, crews set to work cladding their outgunned and out-armoured Sherman tanks in lengths of track over the front, back, and sides to act as armour and deflect enemy shot. Nothing, however, could be done to improve the inadequate guns arming the tanks.

General Simonds orchestrated a formidable convoy. On both sides of the Caen-Falaise highway, armoured vehicles advanced in columns over the crest of Verrières Ridge, each column four vehicles abreast, led by a gapping force composed of two troops of Sherman tanks, two troops of mine-clearing flail tanks, and a troop of AVREs (Assault Vehicle, Royal Engineers) to mark the route with tape and lights. The infantry battalion rode in "unfrocked priests"[33] (universal carriers). A fortress force of mortars, medium machine guns, anti-tank guns, bulldozers, and more tanks completed each phalanx.[34]

The 28th Armoured Brigade (British Columbia and Algonquin Regiments), part of the 4th Canadian Armoured Division, received orders on August 9 to advance toward an objective called Point 195, five kilometres southwest of Bretteville-sur-Laize. But in the poor early morning light and unfamiliar country, with few landmarks, the brigade lost its way. One troop got close to the objective, but the main body turned in the opposite direction to high ground fifteen hundred metres east of Estrées-la-Campagne. The brigade commander, Lieutenant-Colonel Donald Grant Worthington of the BC Regiment, thinking his troop had reached their objective, waited for reinforcements but instead encountered the 12th SS Panzers. The outnumbered Canadians put up a hard fight. Forty officers and men were killed, including Worthington, thirty-four men taken prisoner, and forty-seven tanks lost. The few survivors escaped to Allied lines held by Polish troops. Point 195, in fact, already had been taken by the Argyll and Sutherland Highlanders. In a silent night attack,

the men had marched in single file up the slope of the hill to its top and dug in without arousing the Germans. The next morning they had successfully beat off a series of counterattacks.[35]

La Cambe. Grave of Hauptsturmfuhrer Michael Wittmann and members of his Tiger tank destroyed, possibly, by the Sherbrooke Fusiliers Regiment, 2nd Canadian Armoured Brigade, August 8, 1944. (Susan Evans Shaw)

Right: Normandy, Falaise castle, birthplace of William the Conqueror. (Susan Evans Shaw)

Bottom right: Estrées-la-Campagne, Normandy. Monument to the Worthington Force of 40 officers and men killed at Hill 140 on August 9, 1944, in Phase Two of Operation Totalize. (Susan Evans Shaw)

Totalize lasted four days, ending August 11. In that time, the Canadians fought their way forward along the Caen-Falaise road from Verrières fourteen kilometres toward Falaise, an operation that cost six hundred Canadian dead but the enemy over three thousand. Along the way, mistakes happened. RAF Bomber Command struck at Quesnay Woods and Potigny, but unfortunately some navigators misidentified their targets and ordered the bombing of Canadian and Polish troops in the rear areas. One hundred and fifty died and 241 were wounded, and for a time the ensuing chaos among the remaining troops kept them from the job at hand. More seriously, Montgomery, in command of the overall battle, made a strategic error in failing to use American divisions to trap the Germans in a rapidly forming pocket that might have achieved total victory in Normandy. His mistaken belief that the British and Canadians could close the pocket from the north gave large elements of the German army the chance to escape.[36]

The next stage, the capture of Falaise, ended August 17, but only after a costly battle that left the town, birthplace of William the Conqueror, in ruins. Les Fusiliers Mont-Royal had the job of mopping up the last resistance, a desperate group of fifty or sixty fanatical Hitler Youth. Two or three escaped, and the rest fought to the end. None surrendered.[37]

Getting to the Cemeteries and Memorials

Bretteville-sur-Laize Canadian War Cemetery (p. 158). Most of those buried here died in the battles for Caen, Verrières, and Falaise. Of the 2,958 burials, 2,792 are Canadian, 87 unidentified.

By car: From Caen's peripheral highway, N814, take exit 13 onto N158, direction Alençon/Le Mans/Falaise, and continue for about 8 kilometres. Take exit La Jalousie toward Bretteville-sur-Laize and merge onto D23A. After 320 metres, turn left onto D23; take the first right onto D80 and right again onto D183A. After 2 kilometres, turn right onto D183, then again right onto D167. The cemetery is 650 metres on the right.

Hell's Corner, roughly ten kilometres north of Caen, is marked by a monument to the 9th Canadian Brigade. The monument, a roughly tapered structure of stone and mortar adorned with a plaque, stands at the side of D22 at the western exit of Caen. The intersecting side road has been named rue des Glengarrians. The point marked as Place Hell's Corner at Villons-les-Buissons is now the site of Archives Services Calvados.

By car: From Caen, take N814, then D79 north for about 5 kilometres; turn left onto D220, and continue for 1.9 kilometres and turn right.

Château d'Audrieu. The place where the

Villons-les-Buissons, Normandy. Hell's Corner Memorial to the Canadian 9th Brigade soldiers who fought in this area from June 7 to July 7, 1944. (Susan Evans Shaw)

Château d'Audrieu
(Susan Evans Shaw)

Right: A stele with plaque that reads "In memory of those members of the Royal Winnipeg Rifles and supporting arms who were murdered while prisoners of war, at the Château d'Audrieu near Le Mesnil-Patry and at Le Haut du Bosq on 8, 9 and 11 June 1944." (Susan Evans Shaw)

men from the Royal Winnipeg Rifles, the Cameron Highlanders of Ottawa, the 3rd Anti-Tank Regiment, Royal Canadian Artillery, and the 6th Field Company, Royal Canadian Engineers, were murdered by the 12th SS Panzer Division *Hitlerjugend* is now a luxury hotel. The memorial to the murdered soldiers, a stele of white marble, now much weathered and eroded, and featuring a mounted plaque, is in the nearby village of Audrieu.

By car: From Caen, take N814/E48 and exit onto N13. Head west for 8.7 kilometres. Take D217 exit toward Putot-en-Bessin/Secqueville-en-Bessin. At the roundabout take the fourth exit to D217. Go through one roundabout. Turn right onto D94 then left onto D82. Take the second left onto Château d'Audrieu. The Château is at the end of the road.

Hill 67 Verrières Ridge Canadian Memorial (p.157) is located one kilometre north of St-Martin-de-Fontenay on the D562A. A narrow road on the right, Le Grand Barberie, climbs to the top of the hill where the monument stands. The memorial includes plaques commemorating the Black Watch (Royal Highland Regiment) of Canada, Régiment de Maisonneuve, and the Toronto Scottish Regiment.

Abbaye d'Ardenne, located on the western outskirts of Caen in the district of St-Germain-la-Blanche-Herbe, remains a monastery closed to the public except for the Memorial Garden honouring the eighteen murdered soldiers.

By car: Follow rue d'Authie (D220C) to the roundabout and take the third exit onto rue du Régiment du 1er Hussard. Continue onto rue d'Ardennes. The Abbaye is on the left.

The **Worthington Memorial** to "a tragic mixture of gallantry and ineptitude"[38] stands at the edge of D131, between Estrées-la-Campagne and Maizières, at the intersection with the Soignolles-Rouvres road.

Top left: The Memorial Garden at the Abbaye d'Ardennes. (Susan Evans Shaw)

Above: Normandy, Estrées-la-Campagne. The Worthington Memorial. (Susan Evans Shaw)

Pursuit across the Seine, August 23-30, 1944

The failures of the past eleven weeks had badly damaged the morale of the German Army officer corps. To be driven out of Normandy with such heavy losses underlined their private conviction that the war was lost. Hitler's interference with operations and refusal to accept his commanders' recommendations worsened the situation. On July 20, a group of officers made an attempt on Hitler's life, but the plot failed. The courage of despair now sustained the German armies.[39]

Meanwhile, the Allies struggled forward without access to coastal ports. As their armies moved inland, lines of supply back to the Normandy beaches lengthened by the hour. To add to their problems, the Allies lacked manpower. Infantry casualties in Normandy had been much higher than anticipated. For Canadian commanders, reinforcements were to be a serious source of anxiety throughout the summer and autumn until Mackenzie King could be persuaded to mobilize the conscripts (known as "Zombies") at home in Canada.

Initially, the Canadians received orders to capture the port of Le Havre, but before they could get under way, a new directive arrived from Montgomery to clear the sites in the Pas de Calais of the V-1 flying bombs that had been plaguing London since June 12.[40] Montgomery ordered the First Canadian Army to secure the port of Dieppe and then destroy enemy forces along the coast through Calais as far as Bruges, in Belgium.[41] The Second Canadian Army was to push across the Seine to establish itself in the area of Arras-Amiens-St. Pol, then carry on to Belgium.

On August 27, infantry of the 4th Canadian Division attempted to cross the Seine east of Rouen at Criquebeuf-sur-Seine but were repulsed with heavy losses. A second try the next day succeeded a few kilometres west at Elbeuf, where the enemy had fewer troops to keep them out of the low-lying river loop. Once across the river, the Royal Engineers managed to complete a Bailey pontoon bridge capable of carrying tanks.

At the Forêt de la Londe, a thickly wooded patch in a river oxbow, the 2nd Canadian Division met heavy German opposition. For three days, the enemy fought hard and skilfully from well-camouflaged positions on the river heights. Then, on August 30, resistance let up; the Germans had withdrawn in a great body. Their main purpose had been to hold up the Allied advance while they got as many vehicles as possible across the river. Rouen fell on August 30 to the 2nd Canadian Corps, who were given a tremendous welcome by the French population.

Clearing the Coastal Belt and Ports

> Field Marshal Montgomery issued another directive . . . Canadian Army will clear the coastal belt, and will then remain in the general area Bruges-Calais until the maintenance situation allows of its employment further forward.[42]

After the Seine came the Somme, the next formidable obstacle for the advancing Allies. Between the two great rivers, the British and Canadians made the swiftest advance of the entire campaign. Their worst anxieties now centred on the steadily increasing length of the lines of supply, the solution to which lay in the capture of Channel ports. During World War I, the Germans failed to capture these ports in their "Race to the Sea," and the result was static fighting inland. In 1940, however, they had made it to the sea, and now the problem for the Allies became one of dislodging them. But it wouldn't be easy.

Forgoing a hoped-for rest, the weary Canadians followed orders to continue their progress north. By September 2, the 4th Armoured Car Regiment (12th Manitoba Dragoons) reached the Somme east of Pont Remy while the 2nd Division reached Abbeville. At Dieppe, the Canadians anticipated a hard fight; instead, they found the Germans had already departed. A planned RAF bomb attack was hastily called off, and the Canadians enjoyed an enthusiastic welcome from the overjoyed townspeople. Destruction of the port had not been as extensive as feared. British engineers could set to work preparing the harbour to receive shipping and badly needed supplies while the Canadian 2nd Division paused to refit.[43]

Hitler had designated certain French ports as "fortresses" to be protected and defended to the last. Among them were Brest in Brittany (now besieged by the Americans), Lorient, St-Nazaire, La Rochelle on the Biscay coast (a useless waste of German troops as these ports were of little military value to the Allies), the Channel Islands (again a waste of a good German infantry division), Le Havre, Boulogne, and Dunkirk (vitally necessary to the Allies and heavily defended by the Germans). On September 4, Hitler issued orders to prevent the Allies from reaching Antwerp, but he was too late. The British Second Army had already captured Belgium's capital, Brussels, and Antwerp, the greatest port in Northwest Europe. But although the city's near-intact dock installations were in Allied hands, they could not gain the use of the harbour. Antwerp lies eighty kilometres from the sea, on the Scheldt River estuary, both banks of which remained in German hands.[44]

Meanwhile, Montgomery hatched a new scheme, called Operation Market Garden, which was intended to capture the Dutch town of Arnhem and establish a bridgehead across the lower Rhine, but the operation failed. The bridgehead was not secured, and possibly the only hope of capturing the Ruhr and Berlin in 1944 was lost. Market Garden did secure other objectives of value to later operations, however, as crossings of the Rivers Maas and Waal would serve as a corridor for a later advance to the Rhine.[45]

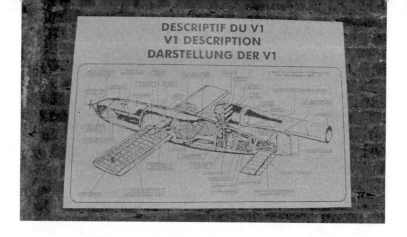

DESCRIPTIF DU V1
V1 DESCRIPTION
DARSTELLUNG DER V1

The Cinderella Army

The moniker [Cinderella Army] derives from its role on the 'long left flank' of the Allies, fighting what seemed like low-priority, attritional battles far from the limelight of the victorious sweeps through France, Belgium, and ultimately, Germany. The Canadians were not invited to the ball.[46]

On September 6, following the refit at Dieppe, the Canadian 2nd Division set about its task. The ports of Le Havre, Boulogne, Calais, and Dunkirk had to be rid of occupying German forces as quickly as possible. The Canadians captured Le Havre on September 11, only to discover that the Germans had systematically demolished the harbour; shipping there would not begin until October 9. The next port, Boulogne,

Top: Val Ygot. V-1 rocket diagram.
(Susan Evans Shaw)

Left: Val Ygot. Bomb crater. (Susan Evans Shaw)

fell on September 22 after six days of hard fighting, but again the enemy's demolition and Allied bomb damage delayed the use of the port until October 12. Calais surrendered on September 30, and to no one's surprise, the Canadians found the Germans had painstakingly razed the port installations. It was November before the harbour could be reopened.

In the interim, the 9th Brigade set about searching for the enemy's cross-Channel batteries and V-1 launching sites. A complex system of minefields, electric fences, bunkers, and anti-tank positions protected the massive installations. Heavy bomber attacks helped clear the way for the Canadian infantry, who put an end to the plague of V-1 rocket attacks on Southeast England.

Getting to the Cemeteries and Memorials

Calais Canadian War Cemetery is located at Leubringhen, 15 kilometres southwest of Calais. Of the 674 burials here, there are 581 Canadians, 6 Czechs, 19 Poles, and 30 unidentified.

By car: In Calais, from the Place du Soldat Inconnu—where the famous sculpture by Rodin, *The Burghers of Calais*, stands—and the Mairie, turn right onto rue Paul Bert then right again onto the Quai de la Gendarmerie. At the roundabout take the second exit to Quai de l'Yser,

Calais Canadian War Cemetery and Cross of Sacrifice.
(Commonwealth War Graves Commission)

which will turn slightly left and become rue Watteau. Make a slight right onto rue Delaroche, then the first right onto boulevard de l'Égalité, then the first left onto rue du Lieutenant Jacques Faguer. Take a slight right onto boulevard Victor Hugo and at the roundabout take the second exit onto the A16 ramp, direction Tunnel sous la Manche/Boulogne/Rouen/Marquise, and merge onto the A16. Continue for about 10 kilometres to exit 38 toward St-Inglevert/Wissant/Cap Gris-Nez. Turn left onto D244E1 and go through one roundabout, then turn left to stay on D244E1/rue de Mauleville. The cemetery is on the left, a neat rectangle set about fifty metres back from the road. The cross of sacrifice is clearly visible.

Calais Southern Cemetery. A total of 880 identified burials are here. Of the 224 World War II burials, 5 are Canadian. There are also twenty-eight Canadian World War I burials from the No. 10 Canadian Stationary Hospital stationed nearby.

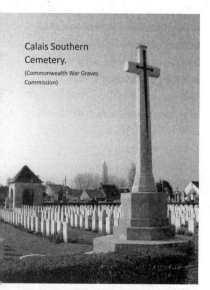

Calais Southern Cemetery.
(Commonwealth War Graves Commission)

By car: From the Place du Soldat Inconnu in Calais, turn right onto rue Paul Bert, then right again onto Quai de la Gendarmerie. At the roundabout, take the third exit onto avenue Louis Blériot. Continue for one kilometre to rue de Mauberge/D119 and turn right. At the Pont de l'Enceinte, turn left and continue onto avenue Antoine de Saint-Exupéry. The cemetery is four hundred metres on the right. The CWGC war graves are in a section at the southeast corner.

Boulogne Eastern Cemetery is 19 kilometres south of Leubringhen and Calais Canadian War Cemetery. There are nearly 5,600 burials here from World War I and 224 from World War II. Of the 17 World War II Canadian burials, 9 are of men killed at Dieppe, the rest are RCAF.

By car: From Calais merge onto the A16, direction Marquise/Boulogne, and travel south 14.5 kilometres to exit 32 toward Boulogne Centre. At the roundabout, take the third exit to the D96E ramp toward Boulogne Centre/St-Martin-Boulogne and merge onto D96E. At the roundabout, take the second exit to D96 and continue onto Route de Calais, which becomes avenue Charles de Gaulle. At the roundabout, take the third exit onto avenue de Lattre de Tassigny. Turn right onto rue Framery, then left onto rue de Dringhen. The large communal cemetery, divided into two parts by the road, is 250 metres on the right. The CWGC military cemetery is a long narrow strip along the west border of the south section.

Val Ygot V-1 Rocket Site/V-1 Stellung Val Ygot

is concealed in the Forêt Domaniale d'Eawy, thirty-four kilometres southeast of Dieppe.

By car: At Dieppe from the D927/avenue de Beauté roundabout, take the third exit to N27/avenue des Canadiens. Continue on N27 for 1.8 kilometres to a roundabout. Take the second exit onto D915 and continue for about 25 kilometres, passing through two roundabouts. Make a sharp right onto D12/

Val Ygot. Ardouval, Normandy. Site of V-1 Rocket, the only rocket site open to the public.
(Susan Evans Shaw)

Route de la Heuzé, and continue onto D99 for 2.8 kilometres. A large sign in the parking area is clearly visible from the road. The rocket launchers can be found after an easy walk through the wood.

Schoonselhof Cemetery, Antwerp, is a community cemetery with the military section toward the back. The cemetery is notable for the lush growth of varied and beautiful trees. Of the 1,437 World War II burials here, 346 are Canadian.

By car: From Antwerp ring-road R1, exit onto A12 heading southwest. Exit onto R11/Gaston Fabrelaan to Krijgsbaan. To get to the cemetery entrance, exit onto Sint Bernardsesteenweg/ N148 south, then take the first left on Krijgsbaan/R11. The cemetery entrance is on the right.

The Battle of the Scheldt

> The North Shores captured a German major who talked of what he called the "Canadian SS Troops": "We can handle the Yanks and the Limeys within reason," he said, "but you Canadians come at us at night with flame throwers, mortars, machine guns, everything — yelling like hell. And you simply terrify our troops."[47]

To open the port of Antwerp to shipping, the Fifteenth German Army had to be cleared from its hold on both banks of the Scheldt estuary. As it was, supply lines for the Allied army stretched from Normandy nearly to the German border, a time- and personnel-consuming burden that risked exhausting fuel, munitions, and men as the Allies advanced. After the delay brought about by the failed Operation Market Garden, Montgomery now made opening of the Scheldt estuary top priority.

Under the command of Lieutenant-General Guy Simonds, the 21st Army Group, supported by the 1st Polish Armoured Division, launched a massive operation on October 2, 1944. Fierce opposition by the enemy caused Simonds to implement the operation in four phases: drive north from Antwerp, clear the Breskens Pocket, advance across South Beveland against Walcheren Island, and begin operations against Walcheren. The

2nd Canadian Infantry Division began the advance north from Antwerp on October 2. On the eve of battle, the 5th Infantry Brigade (Black Watch [Royal Highland Regiment] of Canada, Le Régiment de Maisonneuve, and Calgary Highlanders) enlarged the bridgehead over the Turnhout-Antwerp Canal and captured the village of Brecht. From this position, the South Saskatchewan Regiment occupied Lochtenberg while, pushing steadily north, the 6th Brigade (Les Fusiliers Mont-Royal, Queen's Own Cameron Highlanders of Canada, and South Saskatchewan Regiment) captured Camp de Brasschaet, then occupied Kappellen. After stiff fighting, the Canadians crossed the Dutch frontier on October 5, and the next day took Santvliet, then Ossendrecht. Woensdrecht, their objective for this phase, seemed within grasp, but it took nine days of hard fighting with many casualties before the village finally fell.

Operation Switchback

> To confound the Allies, the Germans, as they had done elsewhere, flooded large tracts of Breskens Pocket, rendering the polders impassable to tracked vehicles and even to foot soldiers. An RCASC [Royal Canadian Army Service Corps] officer noted that the cobblestones would actually sink under the weight of the wheels of heavy supply trucks, then bob up again, giving the impression that the trucks were "riding on soup," Then came a new enemy, the October rains, relentlessly pounding the land and those upon it. Even the areas not inundated became quagmires of mud. It was a wretched land.[48]

Polder country, land reclaimed from the sea, was far from ideal for military operations. Unsuitable for tanks, the burden of battle fell on the infantry. Artillery gave strong support and, weather permitting, so did the Air Force. Engineers too played an important role, constructing bridges and other means of access over the inhospitable terrain.

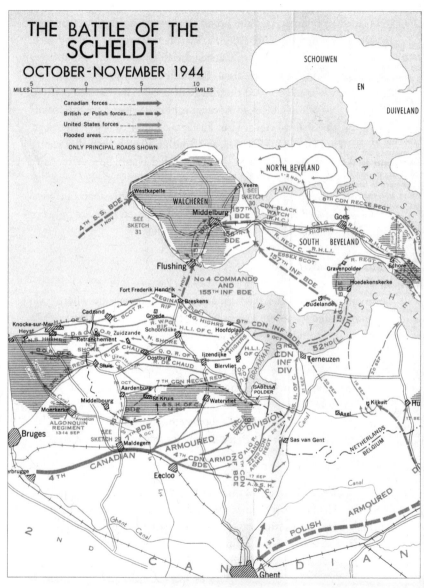

THE BATTLE OF THE SCHELDT
OCTOBER–NOVEMBER 1944

MILES 5 0 5 10 MILES

Canadian forces
British or Polish forces
United States forces
Flooded areas

ONLY PRINCIPAL ROADS SHOWN

SCHOUWEN
EN
DUIVELAND

NORTH BEVELAND
1–2 NOV

Westkapelle
WALCHEREN
Veere
SEE SKETCH 30
157TH BDE
Middelburg
CDN BLACK WATCH (R.H.C.)
4TH S.S. BDE
1 NOV
SEE SKETCH 31
Flushing
Fort Frederik Hendrik
No 4 COMMANDO AND 155TH INF BDE

Goes
8TH CDN RECCE REGT
SOUTH BEVELAND
CALG HIGHRS
R.H.C. R.H.L.I.
R. REGT C.
Schore
R.H.L.I.
Gravenpolder
Hoedekenskerke
Oudelande
157TH INF BDE
Essex Scot
R. REGT C.
156TH BDE
52ND (L) DIV

Breskens
REGINA RIF
C. SCOT R.
Cadzand
Groede
O.R. HIGHRS
R. WPG RIF
Schoondijke
Hoofdplaat
N. SHORE R.
H.L.I. OF C.
9TH CDN INF BDE
9 OCT
Knocke-sur-Mer
Heyst
H.L.I. OF C.
S.D. & G.
R. de Zuidzande
Retranchement
N. SHORE R.
R. DE CHAUD
Oostburg
R. DE CHAUD
Sluis
Q.O.R. OF
Ijzendijke
H.L.I. OF C.
NTH HIGHRS
3RD CDN INF DIV
Terneuzen
52ND (L) DIV
Biervliet
BRAAKMAN

7TH CDN RECCE REGT
Aardenburg
Middelbourg
St. Kruis
Watervliet
ISABELLA POLDER
A. & H. OF C.
14 OCT
8TH BDE
9 OCT
Moerkerke
ALGONQUIN REGIMENT
13–14 SEP
SEE SKETCH 29
Maldegem
7TH BDE
8 OCT
LINC & WELLD
DIVISION
A. & H.O. OF C.
20 SEP
Sas van Gent
Axel
Kijkuit
Hu
NETHERLANDS
BELGIUM

Bruges
erbrugge
4TH CANADIAN
ARMOURED
4TH CDN ARMD BDE
22ND CDN ARMD REGT
Eecloo
17 SEP
A. & S.H. OF C.
ARMOURED
POLISH
1ST POLISH ARMOURED
Ghent Canal
Canal

2 N D C A N A D I A N

Ghent
Lys
Ghent Canal

Source: C.P. Stacey, *Official History of the Canadian Army in the Second World War.*
Volume III: The Victory Campaign: The Operations in North-West Europe, 1944–1945
(Ottawa: Queen's Printer, 1966), map 8.

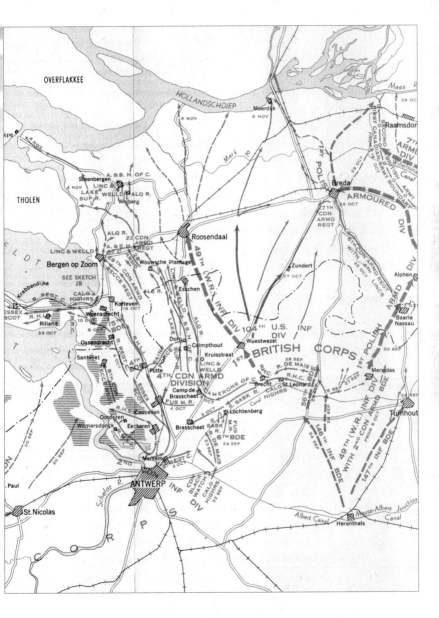

The Canadians in Northwest Europe 187

The attack on the Breskens Pocket began at the only place on the German front not a deep water barrier. At the east end of the German defensive line, there was a gap in the vicinity of the Isabella Polder, between the end of the Leopold Canal and the Braakman Inlet. Unfortunately, it was well fortified, and a first Canadian attempt on the gap ended in failure. Undeterred, the 7th Brigade organized a crossing of the Leopold Canal at the west end near Eede. With heavy losses the brigade crossed the canal, established a bridgehead, and cut off the enemy's ammunition route in the process. Meanwhile an amphibious attack from Terneuzen on the West Scheldt took the enemy by surprise. The Canadian 9th Infantry Brigade landed unopposed at Green Beach, a few kilometres from the coastal village of Hoofdplaat. Step by step the Canadians took possession of the Breskens Pocket, bringing the whole operation to completion by November 2.[49]

Operation Vitality

> What the survivors remembered most was the condition of the battlefield, with its flooded polders and cold, endless rain.[50]

The capture of Breskens and Fort Frederik Hendrik provided the Allies with positions from which artillery could be brought into action against Walcheren Island.[51] But first South Beveland had to be taken. On October 23, the 2nd Canadian Infantry Division began the final clearing of Woensdrecht preparatory to operations. The next day the 4th Brigade began the advance to South Beveland across the isthmus between the East and West Scheldt.[52] The opening gambit started with tanks and reconnaissance cars, but a well-placed anti-tank gun made the operation one for the infantry to be carried out after nightfall. As the Canadians approached the Beveland Canal, which bisects the isthmus, the time came for an amphibious attack across the West Scheldt. The British 52nd (Lowland) Division, supported by an artillery bombardment, landed successfully on two beaches. In combination with the Canadians attacking along the isthmus, they outflanked the German defenders at the canal.

By October 29, South Beveland's capital, Goes, had been taken. By October 31, enemy bunkers at the east end of the Walcheren Causeway were cleared. A minor operation against North Beveland followed, blocking the enemy from escaping by sea. The conquest of South and North Beveland by the combined British and Canadian forces wound up by November 2.

A mere strip of road and railway line, eleven hundred metres by thirty-six metres, joined Walcheren Island to South Beveland. Running arrow-straight through reed-grown mud flats, the Walcheren Causeway offered no cover from the heavy defence by the Germans at the western end. At its midpoint, the causeway had been cratered to make it impassable to tanks and vehicles.

Lieutenant-General Charles Foulkes ordered the Canadian 5th Brigade to establish a bridgehead on Walcheren.[53] A first attempt by the Black Watch to cross the causeway met with heavy fire and many casualties. The Calgary Highlanders renewed the attack, but they too were repulsed. Le Régiment de Maisonneuve (the Maisies) made the third and last attempt. One company managed to get behind the German defence line and hold two positions, one a farmhouse they used as headquarters and the other a railway underpass some 450 metres west of the end of the causeway. There they remained for the next eight hours, totally isolated, fighting with extraordinary courage until they were relieved by elements of the Glasgow Highlanders.[54] Under cover of smoke, the Maisies made their escape, the last troops of the 2nd Canadian Division to be engaged in the Battle of the Scheldt. The 5th Brigade withdrew to a long overdue rest at Mechelen, twenty-five kilometres south of Antwerp. British forces finished rooting out the enemy in the Scheldt estuary in early November, and minesweeping of the Scheldt began November 4. By November 26, the operation was complete, and a few days later the first convoy entered the harbour at Antwerp. The supply stage was now set for the advance into Germany.

Bergen op Zoom Canadian War Cemetery
(Commonwealth War Graves Commission)

Getting to the Cemeteries and Memorials

Bergen op Zoom Canadian War Cemetery
The town of Bergen op Zoom is 143 kilometres south of Amsterdam and 41 kilometres north of Antwerp. Of the 1,087 identified burials here, 967 are Canadian.

By car: From Antwerp, take exit 28 Bergen op Zoom to A58/E312/Rijksweg direction Rooseveltlaan. Exit 28 turns left to become Rooseveltlaan. After five hundred metres, turn right onto Gagelboslaan, then right again onto Wouwestraatweg. Continue onto Ruytershoveweg, which crosses under the A4. The cemetery is one kilometre on the left. From Amsterdam, on the A58, take exit 26-Heerle toward Bergesbaan and turn left onto Bergesbaan, which continues into Ruytershoveweg. The cemetery is 1.3 kilometres on the right.

Flushing (Vlissingen) Northern Cemetery is located on the southern edge of the island of Walcheren, which, because of post-war land reclamation, is technically no longer an island. Of the 178 World War II burials, 32 are Canadian, all members of the RCAF.

By car: From Middelburg, head south on the Nieuw Vlissingseweg/N661 for three kilometres to President Rooseveltlaan. Turn right onto President Rooseveltlaan, then right onto Industrieweg. The cemetery is on the right. From the mainland, take the A58 to Vlissingen. At Vlissingen, continue onto Sloeweg/N288 and take the exit to Nieuw Vlissensweg/N661. Five hundred metres farther on, turn right onto President Rooseveltlaan and again right onto Industrieweg.

November 1944-February 1945

> In those violent weeks of fighting during the Battle of the Scheldt, the men at the front soon witnessed what they came to acknowledge as Canada's blackest disgrace. Political games were being played with human stakes on Europe's battlefields in October, 1944, and Canadian soldiers were the losers.[55]

Exhausted Canadians, badly in need of a break, welcomed the lull that followed the Battle of the Scheldt, a static period that would last until the opening of the Battle of the Rhineland on February 8.

While soldiers at the front rested, back home in Canada political turmoil raged in the controversy over growing demands for reinforcements. Divisional losses due to casualties had been significant while the supply of trained replacements dwindled, even though seventy thousand trained soldiers, conscripted for home defence only, remained on the other side of the Atlantic under the protection of the National Resources Mobilization Act. Under the mistaken conviction of officials in London that the war was winding down, Ottawa saw no need to replace the heavy casualties of the battles in Normandy. Meanwhile, at the front, replacements were being drawn from among the infantry "tradesmen"—cooks, shoemakers, truck drivers, and clerks—men who lacked training as fighting troops and who were thus a danger to themselves and to the more experienced soldiers serving at their side.[56]

For Mackenzie King, the dreaded spectre of conscription hovered over all discussion. Defence Minister J.L. Ralston toured the battlefields of Italy and Northwest Europe and returned to Canada to report on the urgent need for trained men from the home defence units. Mackenzie King, though, chose to remove the messenger and ignore the message. He fired Ralston and replaced him with McNaughton, who assured the prime minister that he could find sufficient volunteers, but a cross-country recruiting mission yielded fewer than six hundred men. Eventually, Mackenzie King bowed to pressure, and sixteen thousand home conscripts were ordered sent overseas.[57] Of these, however, more than two-thirds deserted or went absent without leave before they even left the country. In the end, only twenty-five hundred of the conscripts reached operational units, too late to relieve the troops serving in the Battle of the Scheldt.[58]

While turmoil raged among the Canadians over reinforcements, another controversy heated up in the middle of December between the British and American commands. For a better chance of decisive results, Montgomery advocated for Allied concentration and a massed assault toward the Ruhr, but American generals Bradley and Patton insisted on a policy of dispersion over a broad front that extended from the Swiss border to Maastricht in Belgium. General Eisenhower, the Supreme Allied Commander, but out of his depth as a field commander, hesitated for days while trying to find a solution to please everyone. Meanwhile, Hitler had plenty of time to regroup his armies and organize for a massive attack through the Ardennes.

The war dragged on into 1945.

Top: Abbaye d'Ardennes, Normandy. Part of the memorial to the 18 men of the North Nova Scotia Highlanders and Sherbrooke Fusiliers of the 2nd Armoured Brigade who were executed in cold blood by the *Hitlerjugend.* (Susan Evans Shaw)

Right: Val Ygot. "Hommage aux Victimes 1943-1944." Memorial to the civilian victims of the V-1 rocket attacks. (Susan Evans Shaw)

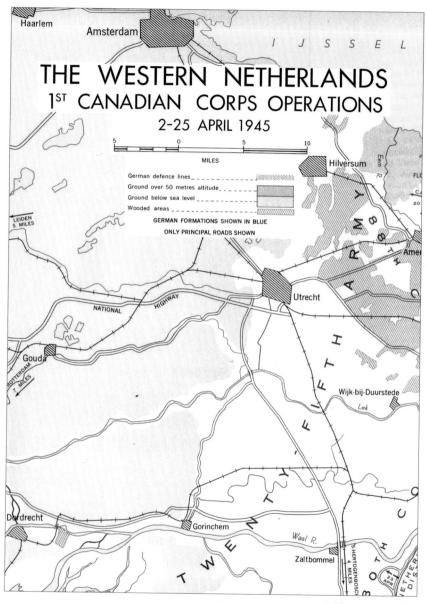

THE WESTERN NETHERLANDS
1ST CANADIAN CORPS OPERATIONS
2–25 APRIL 1945

MILES

German defence lines _ _ _ _ _ _ _ _ _ _ _
Ground over 50 metres altitude _ _ _ _ _ _ _ _
Ground below sea level _ _ _ _ _ _ _ _ _ _ _
Wooded areas _ _ _ _ _ _ _ _ _ _ _ _ _ _ _ _

GERMAN FORMATIONS SHOWN IN BLUE

ONLY PRINCIPAL ROADS SHOWN

Haarlem

Amsterdam

I J S S E L

Hilversum

FL

Eem R.

Leiden 5 MILES

NATIONAL HIGHWAY

Utrecht

Ame

F I F T H   A R M Y   8 8 T H   C

Gouda

ROTTERDAM 7 MILES

Wijk-bij-Duurstede

Lek

Dordrecht

Gorinchem

Waal R.

Zaltbommel

T W E N T Y   F I F T H

B O T H   C

S-HERTOGENBOSCH 4 MILES

NETHER

23 APR

Source: C.P. Stacey, *Official History of the Canadian Army in the Second World War. Volume III: The Victory Campaign: The Operations in North-West Europe, 1944-1945* (Ottawa: Queen's Printer, 1966), map 13.

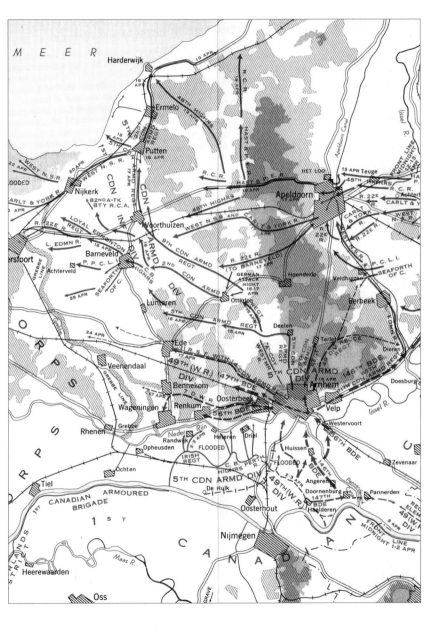

Calais Canadian War Cemetery.
(Commonwealth War Graves Commission)

Val Ygot. Remains of a magnetic building, built without any ferrous material capable of interfering with a magnetic compass. Used for calibrating rocket direction at V-1 launch site. (Susan Evans Shaw)

Right: Cross of Sacrifice
(Susan Evans Shaw)

Below: Juno Beach Centre memorial: "In honour of those who died or disappeared while serving in the Royal Canadian Navy during the conflict of 1939-1945 and in Operation Overlord June 1944. Thank you." (Susan Evans Shaw)

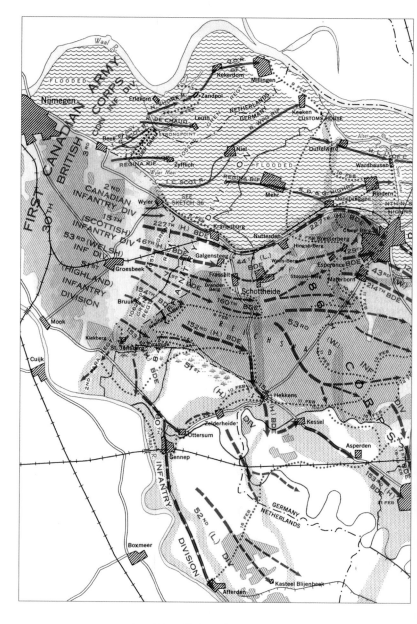

Source: C.P. Stacey, *Official History of the Canadian Army in the Second World War. Volume III: The Victory Campaign: The Operations in North-West Europe, 1944-1945* (Ottawa: Queen's Printer, 1966), map 10.

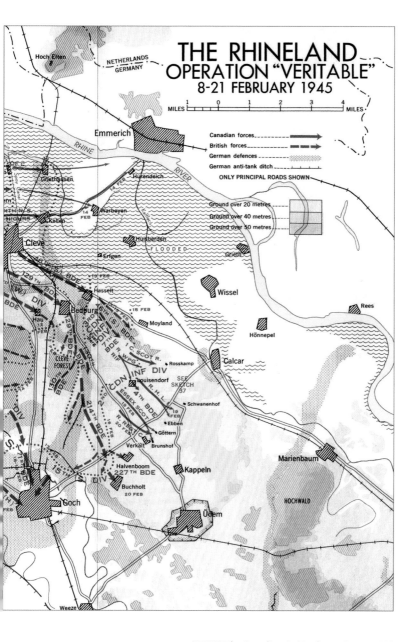

THE RHINELAND
OPERATION "VERITABLE"
8-21 FEBRUARY 1945

MILES 1 0 1 2 3 4 MILES

Canadian forces
British forces
German defences
German anti-tank ditch

ONLY PRINCIPAL ROADS SHOWN

Ground over 20 metres
Ground over 40 metres
Ground over 50 metres

Hoch Elten
NETHERLANDS
GERMANY

Emmerich

RHINE

RIVER

Goethausen

Hurendeich

Warbeyen

14 FEB

Kellen

Cleve

Huisberden

FLOODED

Erlgen

Grieth

Hasselt

Wissel

16 FEB

Bedburg

Rees

Moyland

Hau

Hönnepel

12 FEB

CLEVE
FOREST

C. SCOT. R.

R. WpG

CDN INF DIV

Rosskamp

Calcar

Louisendorf

SEE
SKETCH
37

R.H.L.I.

ESSEX SCOT

CDN INF DIV

Schwanenhof

4 TH BDE

19
FEB

R. REG

Ebben

Göttern

Brunshof

Verkält

Marienbaum

Halvenboom

227 TH BDE

Kappeln

Buchholt

20 FEB

HOCHWALD

Goch

Üdem

Weeze

Top: Memorial to "The Fifty" Allied airmen executed after the "Great Escape", Poznan Old Garrison Cemetery, Poland. (CSvBibra / Wikimedia Commons / Public Domain)

Bottom: Rakowicki Cemetery, Kraków, Poland. (Commonwealth War Graves Commission)

The Battle of the Rhineland

> The Battle of the Rhineland . . . was fought at the sharp end by
> ordinary young men from Britain, Canada and the United States
> who had no ambition to conquer the world or even to save it for
> democracy. By 1945 all that was left was some personal pride and
> the feeling that you should not be the one to quit and let your
> buddies down.[59]

In the middle of December 1944, in what became known as the Battle
of the Bulge, the Germans made a last-ditch attempt to push back the
Americans and advance on Brussels and Antwerp. Hitler's particular
aim was to stabilize the Western Front to free forces for transfer to the
Russian Front. The plan achieved tactical and strategic surprise, but the
Allies ultimately prevailed.

Operation Veritable

No Canadian units were involved in the Battle of the Bulge, but the action
delayed their next operation, Veritable, until February 8. The weather
turned favourable for air support of an artillery bombardment by over
a thousand guns, the prolonged strain of which told on the defending
Germans. The guns did their work so well that the initial attack met with
only light opposition, as the 2nd Canadian Division (now consisting of Le
Régiment de Maisonneuve, Black Watch of Canada, South Saskatchewan
Regiment, Les Fusiliers Mont-Royal, and the Cameron Highlanders
of Ottawa) and three British divisions penetrated into the Reichswald.

Earlier in the winter, the Germans had breached the main dyke at
Eriekom, six kilometres east of Nijmegen. Under pressure from a sudden
thaw and blocked drainage ditches, in addition to the waters released by
the breached dyke, and further weakened by German digging of defensive
trenches, the sixteen-hundred-metre Quer Dam collapsed.[60] Water poured

eastwards, submerging the Canadian 3rd Division area. In consequence, infantry rode to their objectives in amphibious vehicles largely without armoured support. Nevertheless, in the corridor between the northern edge of the Reichswald and the flooded Canadian sector, a combined assault by the 3rd Division and the King's Own Scottish Borderers crossed the West Wall (the infamous Siegfried Line) to finish up at the fringe of Cleve. By February 11, Cleve had fallen to the Allies. The Germans blew more dams and flooding intensified, but the Allied advance went on methodically, sector by sector. By February 21, the Allies had opened the Goch-Kalkar road and pushed the German defenders ever closer to the Rhine.

Operation Blockbuster

On February 26, the 2nd Canadian Corps with two British divisions began an offensive, code-named Blockbuster, to break through to the Hochwald, from there to dislodge the enemy from the Rhineland villages of Xanten, Veen, and Alpen. The operation began with an assault on Kalkar Ridge by the 2nd Canadian Division. The ridge was defended by some of the best troops the enemy possessed, including the 6th Parachute Division and the 47th Panzers. By the morning of February 27, flanked by the British 5th Wiltshire Battalion, the Canadian 2nd Division took the Kalkar portion of the ridge. Nine kilometres to the south, near Uden, the two highest points of the ridge fell to the Canadian 3rd Division (the Queen's Own Rifles, the North Shore [New Brunswick] Regiment, and Le Régiment de la Chaudière). With the first stage of the operation accomplished, the thrust to the Hochwald could now go forward.[61]

A few kilometres to the south, at Mooshof, Sergeant Aubrey Cosens, riding the turret of a Sherman tank, drove forward to clear three obstructive houses full of Germans. He succeeded in killing twenty, took as many prisoners, and enabled the capture of an important objective. A short while later, on the way to report to his commanding officer, he was killed by a sniper's bullet. Sergeant Cosens was awarded a posthumous Victoria Cross. He is buried in Groesbeek Canadian War Cemetery.

The 3rd Division's next task was to complete the capture of Uden, which would clear the way for an advance to the east by the 10th Armoured Division. On February 27, two infantry battalions, the Stormont, Dundas and Glengarry Highlanders and the Highland Light Infantry, advanced on foot across the anti-tank ditch in front of Uden. In the town, they met with stiff resistance from the German 7th Parachute Regiment, but by mid-morning, when they were joined by the North Nova Scotia Highlanders, the 3rd Division occupied Uden.

By March 1, the fighting had moved to the woods east of the town, another task for the infantry. On the left, "C" Company of the Essex Scottish, led by Major Frederick Albert Tilston, assaulted across 450 metres of open ground and through three metres of barbed wire. As the battle wore on, Tilston crossed bullet-swept ground to carry grenades and ammunition to his hard-pressed men, suffering wounds to head and legs in the process. After he collapsed in a shell hole, he refused medical attention until after he had briefed his replacement. Tilston's gallantry cost him both legs but earned him the Victoria Cross.[62]

The Lake Superior Regiment, along with "D" Company of the Algonquins and armoured squadrons of the Governor General's Foot Guards and Canadian Grenadier Guards, fought at the Hochwald gap through devastating fire from well-concealed German tanks. After five days with little rest and scarce hot meals, morale remained high, and by March 4, at a cost of 65 killed and 135 wounded, infantry and tanks succeeded in clearing the wood, opening the way for an assault on enemy positions at Xanten, Veen, and Alpen. Xanten, a Roman town and, in German mythology, the home of Siegfried of Wagnerian opera fame, was targeted in a set-piece operation carried out by the 2nd Division while the 4th Armoured Division fought a "savage slugging match" for Veen.[63] By March 10, after a month of formidable fighting, most German units had been pushed back across the Rhine.

The Battle of the Rhineland was over. Total Allied casualties from February 8 to March 10 numbered 1,049 officers and 14,585 other ranks. Canadian casualties numbered 379 officers and 4,925 other ranks.

Getting to the Cemeteries and Memorials

Reichswald Forest War Cemetery was created after World War II when burials were brought in from surrounding regions to make the largest Commonwealth burial ground in Germany. Of the 7,594 Commonwealth burials of World War II, 704 are airmen of the RCAF and 1 infantryman, Marcel Gagné of Le Régiment de la Chaudière, in a shared grave.

By car: From Cleve/Kleve, driving southeast on the Ringstrasse toward Rütgerstrasse, make a slight left onto Lindenallee, then right onto Hoffmannallee/L484, which becomes Materborner Allee after one kilometre. After another 1.5 kilometres, Materborner Allee becomes Grunewaldstrasse but still L484. Continue for three kilometres to the cemetery on the left side of the road. The Stone of Remembrance and Cross of Sacrifice face the entrance and the burials extend in two long arms on either side.

Rheinberg War Cemetery. Of the 3,326 burials here, mostly Commonwealth airmen, 156 are unidentified, 45 are men of the RCAF, and 9 are Poles.

By car: From Rheinberg, take Bahnhofstrasse/K31/K35 southwest to a T-intersection. Turn left onto K35, still the Bahnhofstrasse, and, at the next intersection, turn right onto B510. Continue for 1.2 kilometres, then turn right at the CWGC sign *Am Englische Friedhof.* The cemetery is 260 metres straight ahead.

Groesbeek Canadian War Cemetery is located in the middle of farmlands approximately 10 kilometres east of Nijmegen. Of the 2,610 Commonwealth burials, 1,296 are of Canadian infantry killed in the Battle of the Rhine.

Groesbeek Memorial stands within the cemetery grounds. Of the 1,034 Commonwealth soldiers named who have no known grave, 100 are Canadian.

By car: From the intersection of Biostraat and Marie Curiestraat in Nijmegen, head east and take the third right onto Nieuw Mollenhutesweg for forty-five metres, then turn left onto Grootstalelaan. After one kilometre and crossing Rijksweg/St. Anne Street, Grootstalselaan becomes Scheidingsweg, then Sionsweg. At the roundabout, take the first exit to Nijmeegsebaan and continue for 2.2 kilometres. At Derdebaan, turn left and, after 1.7 kilometres, turn left onto Zevenheuvenlenweg, taking the first right to the cemetery.

Groesbeek Canadian War
Cemetery Cross of Sacrifice.
(Commonwealth War Graves Commission)

Jonkerbos War Cemetery is less than 2 kilometres from the centre of Nijmegen. Of the 1,532 identified Commonwealth burials, 88 are Canadian airmen of the RCAF.

By car: From Marie Curiestraat and Biostraat, head west to Hatertseweg and turn right. After 550 metres, turn left onto Burgemeester Daleslaan and continue for 1 kilometre. The cemetery is on the left, the graves arranged in a semicircle in the midst of woodland, with the Stone of Remembrance facing the entrance and the Cross of Sacrifice behind at the perimeter.

Uden War Cemetery The town of Uden is roughly halfway between Nijmegen to the north and Eindhoven to the south. Of the 701 Commonwealth burials, 53 are RCAF.

By car: From the north, take A50 direction Rotterdam/Eindhoven to exit 14 direction Uden-Centrum. At the roundabout, take the third exit onto Rondweg, go though one roundabout, and at the next take the first exit to Bitswijk. Go through one roundabout and continue on Monseigneur Bosstraat. Turn left onto Puisplein and continue onto Bergemeester Buskensstraat. The cemetery is on the right at 1 Bergemeester Buskenstraat. From the south, take the A50 to exit 14 and follow the above directions.

The Liberation of Holland

On January 30, 1945, the Combined Chiefs of Staff met at Malta. Eisenhower and Montgomery differed over the tactics of how to proceed with the next stage of the advance into Germany. Montgomery argued for a single front while Eisenhower favoured a two-pronged attack. Principally at issue was the matter of a commander for all Allied ground operations. The Americans resented Montgomery's manner and assumption of authority as Britain and Canada together were contributing only one-quarter of the total Allied force engaged in the European war. As well, they suspected Montgomery of wanting the glory of capturing Berlin for the British Army. The firm hand of General George C. Marshall ended the debate in Eisenhower's favour and the assault over the Rhine went in on two fronts.[64]

The most important consequence of the conference for the First Canadian Army was the decision to withdraw the 1st Canadian Corps from Italy and reunite it with the main body of the field force in Northwest Europe.[65] By April 3, 1945, the entire Corps had arrived in Europe and all the Canadians were together for the last weeks of fighting.[66]

German defenders on the Rhine were woefully undermanned, short of ammunition, and low in morale. Hitler had refused to build defences east of the Rhine and his army had not organized defences in depth. The Germans were also uncertain as to where the river crossing would take place. The Americans had already crossed the southern reaches of the Rhine, but the strongest German opposition was to Montgomery's northern operation. Known as Operation Varsity, parachutists and glider-borne troops were lifted by 1,589 paratroop aircraft and 1,337 gliders. British and American fighter planes provided escort and cover. There was no enemy opposition in the air, but light anti-aircraft guns caused havoc against British glider zones around Hamminkeln. All the same, despite poor visibility at low altitudes, Operation Varsity was a success with both American and British objectives established.[67]

The 1st Canadian Parachute Battalion landed with the 3rd Parachute Brigade west of Hamminkeln on the east bank of the Rhine opposite Xanten. There they met with machine-gun and sniper fire, killing commanding officer Lieutenant-Colonel Jeff Albert Nicklin. Medical orderly Corporal Frederick George Topham won the Victoria Cross for his bravery treating casualties after the drop and, despite being wounded himself, continuing under fire to remove every casualty to safety.

The Highland Light Infantry of Canada received orders to clear the village of Speldrop to open an exit from a pocket formed by a river oxbow, the Alter Rhein, northwest of Rees. The struggle centred on the villages of Grietherbusch, Bienen, and Millingen on either side of the oxbow. The Stormont, Dundas and Glengarry Highlanders took Grietherbusch easily but at Bienen the North Nova Scotia Highlanders were pinned down by the 15th Panzer Grenadier Division, which put up a fierce resistance, prepared to fight to the death. The North Novas eventually captured the village, but the cost in casualties was high. Millingen, northwest of Bienen on the main railway line between Emmerich and Wesel, fell to an attack by the North Shore (New Brunswick) Regiment on March 27. By the beginning of April, three bridges over the Rhine had been completed at Emmerich and five more at Rees in the British sector.

While the British and the Americans raced east to the River Elbe, the Canadians had the less glamorous task of opening up a supply route to the north through Arnhem and Zutphen to maintain forces east of the Rhine.[68] A major obstacle faced the Canadians. The River Ijssel flows due north from the Rhine, its width ranging from 100 to 180 metres, bordered by high flood banks, and the Canadians had to cross it to reach their objective. Moreover, running at right angles, the Twente Canal joins the Ijssel just north of Zutphen, forming a natural line of defence. In a surprise attack, the 2nd Canadian Division, using assault boats, crossed the canal six kilometres east of Zutphen and consolidated a bridgehead. With help from the Dutch underground, the division succeeded in clearing the town of Deventer, while the 8th Canadian Infantry Brigade captured Zutphen.

Operation Cannonshot, April 11-17, 1945

General Crerar, in accordance with Montgomery's directive, made it a top priority to open a route from Arnhem to Zutphen. With Deventer and Zutphen cleared of the enemy, a crossing of the Ijssel from the east and the capture of Apeldoorn became the objective of Operation Cannonshot, launched on April 11.

The 2nd Infantry Brigade (Princess Patricia's Canadian Light Infantry, Loyal Edmonton Brigade, and the Seaforth Highlanders) of the 1st Canadian Infantry Division, newly arrived from Italy, made the assault across the Ijssel under the command of General Simonds. Surprise achieved, the action went according to plan, and in no time engineers had started constructing bridges and rafts to accommodate the follow-up forces. The 1st Infantry Brigade (Royal Canadian Regiment, 48th Highlanders, and Hastings and Prince Edward Regiment) and 3rd Infantry Brigade (Royal 22e Régiment, Carleton and York Regiment, and West Nova Scotia Regiment) made their different approaches to Apeldoorn, each encountering various degrees of resistance by the Germans. An assault on a city full of friendly civilians had to be conducted carefully if unnecessary casualties were to be avoided. Tactical air and artillery assaults were out of the question, so infantry and tanks had to clear out the enemy one house at a time. By April 17, however, the Germans were gone, the city left intact. Casualties over the six-day operation numbered 506, including 100 killed.

The Capture of Arnhem

The British 49th Division, serving with the 1st Canadian Corps, was given the responsibility of the battle for Arnhem. In the event, there was little German resistance, and by April 14, Arnhem had been completely cleared. Following the 49th Division into Arnhem, the 5th Canadian Armoured Division (Lord Strathcona's Horse, 8th Princess Louise's [New Brunswick] Hussars, and the British Columbia Dragoons) used the opportunity to cut off the retreat of Germans fighting on the Apeldoorn canal line. The 1st and 3rd Infantry Brigades continued the drive toward the Ijsselmeer, clearing Otterlo and Barneveld, and finishing up at the German Grebbe Line, a system of fortifications mainly directed toward the sea between the Ijsselmeer and the Neder Rijn that had been built originally in 1940 by the Dutch in an attempt to hold back the invading Germans.

Holland, Grebbe Line, March 2007.
(H. Bot / Wikimedia Commons / CC BY-SA 2.5)

The Problem of Dutch Relief

[T]he Canadians were confronted with a new set of problems. Reports from the old provinces of Holland, including the cities of Amsterdam and Rotterdam, indicated that the terrible conditions of the "hunger winter" were continuing and that the people of western Holland were facing starvation.[69]

For humanitarian reasons, Eisenhower decided the Allies would advance no further, but turn their attention to getting food supplies to the starving civilian population of the Netherlands. In 1944, the Dutch Resistance had called a railway strike against their German occupiers. In retaliation, Reichskommissar Arthur Seyss-Inquart placed an embargo on food supplies from eastern agricultural districts to urban areas in the western Netherlands. Roosevelt and Churchill had assured the Dutch people that help would come after the liberation expected in 1944, but liberation did not come until spring 1945, and a major catastrophe was imminent unless something could be done immediately.

Some relief to occupied Holland was organized through neutral Sweden and the International Red Cross. Finally, an agreement was reached whereby Seyss-Inquart would facilitate supplies of food and coal to the western Netherlands if the First Canadian Army would halt east of the Grebbe Line. In May 1945 the RAF and the USAAF dropped eleven thousand tons of food into occupied western Netherlands, but this aerial

supply proved insufficient, and the Canadians organized Operation Faust — convoys of trucks that delivered one thousand tons of food daily until it ended on May 10, shortly after the German surrender. The Canadians also set to work to re-establish water supplies, electric power, and coal so the Dutch could begin to fend for themselves.

Normandy, France. Juno Beach Centre sculpture, *Remembrance and Renewal*, created by Canadian sculptor Colin Gibson, west-facing aspect. Courseulles-sur-Mer.

(Susan Evans Shaw)

There, in front of the Grebbe Line, the Canadian Corps sat out the final two weeks of the war.[70]

As part of the mopping-up operations, the Canadians were assigned to northern Germany and the capture of Oldenburg and Bremen, after which they were to operate further northwards to capture Emden and Wilhelmshaven. Their final stop was at Delfzijl, the largest secondary port of the Netherlands, which they captured on May 1. By then, much of the enemy force had departed by sea, but the Canadians still managed to take 109 officers and 4,034 other ranks prisoner. All hostilities ceased on May 5, and the formal surrender took place on VE-Day, May 8.

Getting to the Cemeteries and Memorials

Holten Canadian War Cemetery contains 1,393 Commonwealth burials from the last days of World War II, of whom 1,347 are Canadian.

By car: The cemetery is 128 kilometres due east of Amsterdam and can be reached via the A1.E30 about 14 kilometres east of Deventer. Take exit 28 onto N332 northbound to Holten. After about 2 kilometres on N332, bear right onto Laurensweg, which takes you to Holten. Go through one roundabout and turn left onto Dorpstraat; at the roundabout, take the first exit onto Burgemeester van der Borchstraat. Turn right

onto Molenbetterweg for 850 metres to Holterbergweg and turn left, then right after 750 metres onto Wullenbergweg. Continue for 650 metres to Eehornweg. The cemetery is on the left.

Holton Canadian War Cemetery.
(Commonwealth War Graves Commission)

PART VI
Last Things

The Canadians in Sussex

Contrary to expectations, Dunkirk had not been followed up by a German invasion of Britain. In the autumn of 1941, the British commander-in-chief, Sir Alan Brooke, therefore suggested to General McNaughton that the Canadians give up their role of mobile defence and move to stationary defence in Sussex, on the Channel coast south of London.[1] The 2nd Canadian Division accordingly took over there from the 55th British Division. The rest of the Canadian Corps willingly left their uncomfortable Aldershot quarters and, in October 1941, opened new headquarters in Sussex. The Corps area now extended from the Hampshire border near Portsmouth to Fairlight Church, east of Hastings.

Once they were settled, the Canadians began a drastic overhaul of defence arrangements under the operational direction of Montgomery, who lectured the troops on what he called "offensive mentality." Commanded by Harry Crerar, they developed plans on the assumption that an invasion of Britain would be in the form of a combined airborne and seaborne operation. But nothing happened—the enemy never made the smallest attempt against the coasts of England. The Corps held the Sussex coast for more than eighteen months with never a defensive shot fired except at enemy aircraft. On June 3, 1943, operational responsibilities were handed over to the Sussex District Formation, and the 1st Canadian Infantry Division prepared to leave for Italy.

Town of Lewes, Sussex. (Susan Evans Shaw)

Canadian Sappers at Gibraltar
(Source: C.P. Stacey, *Official History of the Canadian Army in the Second World War. Volume I: Six Years of War: The Army in Canada, Britain and the Pacific* (Ottawa: Queen's Printer, 1955), 306)

Canadian Sappers at Gibraltar

After the entry of Italy into the war, Gibraltar became vital to Allied defences.[2] The task of providing long-term accommodation underground fell to Canadian tunnellers brought over by General McNaughton. They arrived at Gibraltar on March 10, 1941 and, in collaboration with three British tunnelling companies, set to work. In the heart of the rock, they excavated a bomb-proof hospital. An east-west tunnel provided direct access with side chambers for laundry. To the south, away from the living and working areas, they worked on two large magazines for storage of ammunition and explosives.

Because the civilian population had been evacuated, Gibraltar became a confined and rather boring station unpopular with the Canadian sappers. Late in 1942, they were happy to be returned to England at last.

The Expedition to Spitsbergen

Concern about the vulnerability of the archipelago of Spitsbergen arose as a minor consequence of the German invasion of the Soviet Union in 1941. Located in the Arctic Ocean north of Scandinavia, the islands, in fact, were Norwegian territory, but the Soviets had interests in the coal mines and in the 2,800 Russian miners who worked there. In addition to the mines, they had established wireless stations which provided the German stations in Norway with weather information, a vital aid to the predatory U-boats. The possibility of German occupation constituted a serious threat to the supply convoy route to Russia.

Canadian Military Headquarters in London had initially proposed to establish a force to protect a naval anchorage and refuelling base until the winter freeze-up. As doubt grew about the plan's feasibility, it was decided to destroy or remove the coal-mining facilities, stocks of coal, harbour facilities, wireless stations, and weather stations. The Russian miners would be repatriated to Archangel, and the resident Norwegians removed to Britain. For the operation, a force of 46 officers and 599 other ranks—including 29 Canadian officers and 498 other ranks, mostly from the Edmonton Regiment, and detachments of Norwegian and British infantry—were moved to Inverary, Scotland, where they embarked on the *Empress of Canada* for Spitzbergen escorted by two cruisers and three destroyers.

Empress of Canada.
(Empress of Canada (1922) by Percy Bentley / British Library, HS85 / 10 / 40306 / Wikimedia Commons / Public Domain)

At Spitsbergen, the force anchored off the village of Barentsberg, and the entire Russian population of the island was taken on board the *Empress of Canada* and transported to Archangel, where the *Empress* picked up 186 escaped French prisoners of war. Meanwhile, sappers got busy and undertook the demolition at Spitsbergen. They set alight piles of coal, poured fuel oil into the sea, and disabled all the mining machinery. When the *Empress* returned, the island's Norwegian population joined the French POWs on board, and the convoy departed on September 6, 1941, leaving Spitsbergen empty of humanity.[3]

To deceive German observers in Norway, a wireless station on Spitsbergen sent out false weather reports until the ships had departed. Only then were all the wireless stations put out of action. For the duration of the war, Spitsbergen remained in Allied hands.

The Canadian Forestry Corps

As in World War I, a Canadian Forestry Corps was formed to chop down European trees, although, after the fall of France in 1940, their labours had to be confined to Britain. Twenty companies, each about two hundred strong, were mobilized and trained in Canada. Initially, they were under the overall command of Brigadier-General J.B. White, who had been in charge of timber operations in 1918. As the war dragged on, the Corps grew to seven thousand all ranks.

Thirteen forestry companies were organized in five "forestry districts" in the Scottish counties of Inverness, Ross, Aberdeen, Nairn, and Perth. The companies worked in two sections, one cutting and bringing out the timber, and the other sawing it into lumber in the company mill using Canadian mechanical equipment. As in the earlier war, a proportion of each forestry unit's time was devoted to military training in preparation for the defence of their area in the event of an invasion.[4]

The Canadian Women's Army Corps

Except for the nursing sisters, Canadian women in World War I served only in civilian capacities. All that changed in World War II. Women made their way into military service as a result both of manpower shortages and their desire to take on a role in their nation's war effort. Having made the decision to enlist female volunteers, the Canadian government set up a new organization on June 27, 1941, designated the Canadian Women's Army Corps (CWAC). Recruiting began in September, and by December 1,256 women had enlisted. At first, the women's corps had different ranks and insignia from the Regular Army, but the system ran into so many administrative difficulties that, in March 1942, the CWAC became a corps of the Active Militia. They now came under military law and assumed Regular Army ranks and badges, but at pay levels two-thirds those of the men, rising to 80 percent in 1943.

The women's military duties in Canada were primarily clerical at National Defence Headquarters. Female junior staff officers replaced male officers as they departed for active duty. Women also served in the Army Show, entertaining troops at home and abroad. Other positions included cooks, drivers, laundrywomen, switchboard operators, cipher operators, and dental assistants. Later, women were employed in gun operations rooms. They served in Washington, D.C., Britain, and at administrative headquarters in Italy and Northwest Europe. In all, 21,624 women served in the CWAC, of whom 1,984 served overseas in the European zone. While no member of the CWAC was killed due to enemy action, four were wounded by a V-2 rocket attack on Antwerp in 1945.

Canadian Women's Army Corps' Cap Badge.
(Mondochrome / Wikimedia Commons / CC BY-SA 3.0)

Many more would have been sent overseas had it not been for the long static period between 1941 and 1944 when men of low medical category were available, making it unnecessary to ship women overseas.

Deadly Weapons: Canada's Chemical and Biological Warfare Program

It was a war of scientist against scientist.[5]

Facing what he perceived as total no-holds-barred war, Nobel laureate Sir Frederick Banting, co-discoverer of insulin, wrote a blueprint in early January 1940 for bacteriological warfare research. His ideas involved infected bullets, disease-carrying insects, and aerial spraying of deadly bacteria.[6] Banting's paper advocated government funding for research to counteract a possible threat from an enemy that in the earlier war had had no compunction about initiating the use of poison gas. A 1925 Geneva Protocol had outlawed the use of chemical and biological weapons. Canada, Britain, and the United States were signatories, but nevertheless desultory research continued even before Britain declared war on Germany in 1939. The next year, Churchill, suspecting the Nazis of similar activity, ordered the military, in defiance of the Protocol, to step up chemical research.

In Canada, a number of eminent scientists were recruited, and in late 1940 construction began on Canada's first poison gas factory, located at Windsor, Ontario. In October 1940, land was found near Medicine Hat, Alberta, to carry out chemical warfare experiments, and Experimental Station Suffield, a "meagre shamble of buildings" located on semi-arid grassland over a vast pool of natural gas, came into existence.[7]

Sir Frederick Banting, however, was on his way to England in February 1941 for secret talks when he died in a plane crash in Newfoundland. His death stalled Canadian research into bacteriological warfare for a time, until a joint meeting of British, American, and Canadian scientists took place in Baltimore at the end of December 1941. The subjects discussed included dissemination of human, animal, and plant diseases and poisoning of food products and water supplies. In the end, neither side in the war resorted to the use of such tactics.

After the war, the Americans claimed all the credit for the work done on chemical and biological weapons, and Prime Minister Mackenzie King would not permit a Canadian report countering the American claims. After the defection of Russian spy Igor Gouzenko in 1945, Mackenzie King's fear of a war with the Soviet Union caused him to clamp a lid of secrecy on Canada's contribution.[8] To this day, very little is generally known about the part Canadians played.

Prisoners of War

[The prisoners] are ordinary people placed in an extraordinary situation as prisoners of war. They found themselves in a tight spot and made the best of it. They did it with a sense of humour; when things got tough they helped one another, they pulled together. At a time when many were mere teenagers or in their early twenties, they displayed a maturity that belied their ages. Their conduct was a credit to their country. And they were so proud to be Canadian.[9]

Most of the Canadians held as prisoners in the early days of the war were airmen, since, until the assault on Dieppe in 1942, the only Allied incursions on Europe were from the air. Should a plane be shot down, survivors found themselves in enemy territory. A few managed to make it to freedom, but the rest were imprisoned in the many POW camps scattered throughout German-occupied territory.[10]

In the aftermath of the disastrous raid at Dieppe, the Germans took prisoner a total of 1,946 Canadians and nearly 400 British officers and enlisted men. Officers were separated from the rest and eventually sent to Oflag VII-B at Eichstatt near Munich. All the Dieppe POWs were marched through the town to Envermeu, many without shoes and wearing only a blanket, having lost their uniforms in the sea. German guards herded the prisoners into an unused brick factory where the restricted space made the sufferings of the wounded all the more acute. Only a single hose provided drinking water, and the food supplied consisted of minute portions of black bread. The plight of the wounded became even more serious as the men were marched to a French prison at Verneulles, twenty kilometres away. Food was bad—only a bucket of watery soup for thirty men and 250 grams of black bread per day. No utensils, blankets, or beds were provided. British Regimental Sergeant-Major Harry Beesley of the No. 3 Commandos took charge. He instructed everyone: "Conduct yourselves as soldiers at all times. Make your enemy respect you. In time they will fear you."[11] From now on they would be fighting an insidious battle of wits with the purpose of hoodwinking their captors.

At the end of five days, the men were marched to the railway station at Verneulles and crowded into small European boxcars, with only a tiny barred window above a man's height providing ventilation. The floor was covered with filthy straw and a single pail in the centre served as a toilet. A ten-gallon milk can provided the sole source of drinking water. Lying down in the crowded space was impossible. Five days and nights of sheer misery ensued before they arrived at Stalag VIII-B at Lamsdorf, near Breslau. It had been the biggest POW camp in Germany in the Great War; its reputation was evil then and remained so now. There, the Canadians joined British prisoners held since Dunkirk.

In early September 1942, German guards were ordered to tie the hands of Canadian prisoners in an act of retaliation. Bodies of Germans had been found with their hands tied, which bore out an operational order found among the papers of an Allied prisoner (see part 3, above) that contained a clause requiring the Dieppe raiders to tie the hands of German prisoners to prevent them destroying documents. Initially, prisoners' hands were tied with string from the Red Cross parcels. Later, handcuffs were used, but the prisoners quickly found that the key from

Canadian prisoners of war being led through Dieppe by German soldiers.
(Library and Archives Canada / C-014171)

Brunswick sardine tins opened the cuffs. As soon as German guards' backs were turned, prisoners would free themselves, re-shackling whenever a guard appeared.[12] Shackling continued until November 1943.

POWs were honour-bound to try to escape, and one of the most famous attempts was made at Stalag Luft III, which housed mainly prisoners of the RAF, RCAF, and, for a time, the USAAF. In the "Great Escape," seventy-six prisoners, including eight Canadians (but no Americans, who had all been shipped out of the camp before the escape), exited from a tunnel. All but three were eventually caught, and fifty were murdered in retribution, either singly or in pairs, among them six of the Canadians.[13]

Unlike Stalag III-B of the Great Escape, where a large group of men made a break for freedom, the tunnels at Stalag VIII-B, which housed some Canadians captured at Dieppe, were used as escape routes for only two men at a time and only for eligible candidates important to the war effort. Somehow, messages got through from the British civil service at Whitehall identifying those prisoners to be given priority for escape. A stipulation for the candidates was that one of the pair had to be fluent in another language. Their departures would be covered by finding look-alikes to take the place of the missing men during roll call. With luck, an absence would not be noticed for days. As a result of these precautions, half of the escapees eventually made it to England. All the same, there was no room for complacency. The men knew they harboured a traitor in their midst, but he was never identified.

In February 1945, as German resistance began to collapse, death marches of prisoners began as POWs were moved from peripheral prison camps to the centre of the country and away from the advancing Russians. Back and forth across Germany, the POWs joined millions of refugees escaping the feared ravages of the Russians. They marched on empty stomachs, as food dumps had been destroyed by Allied bombing. Prisoners survived by stealing. Only twice during the forty-four days the Canadians marched did the Red Cross catch up with life-saving food parcels. Several times prisoners and guards were strafed by Allied aircraft that mistook them for Germans, and many were killed or wounded.[14] By the beginning of May, word of the coming surrender reached prisoners and guards. The guards fled. Eventually, advancing Americans and Russians found the prisoners, who by then were starved, filthy, lousy, and clad mostly in rags. One of the most common first requests was for a bath.[15]

The Canadians who surrendered at Hong Kong were treated particularly brutally. Conditions in the North Point POW camp were so overcrowded that epidemics of dysentery resulted. No sulpha drugs were available for treatment; the Japanese took them for their own use. The dysentery hospital was an old warehouse where men in stretchers lay on the floor. Attempts at escape proved futile, and those caught were shot. Each time someone tried an escape, rations were cut.

Sham Shui Po on the mainland was another such camp. Conditions there were filthy, and men were dying of malnutrition on a diet of plain rice and water. Sometimes the Japanese provided vegetable greens in the form of chrysanthemums, sweet potato tops, potato tops, and buttercups. The prisoners chopped them up to make what they called "green horror" soup. Other variations on the monotonous diet were sprats cooked in soy sauce, and whale or porpoise meat with all the good parts already taken. Prisoners found that eating with chopsticks prolonged their meagre meal. The prisoners were also plagued with diphtheria, beriberi, pellagra, amoebic dysentery, bacillary dysentery, and a swelling of the testicles known as Hong Kong balls. Diphtheria claimed the lives of 50 Canadians, and another 128 succumbed to the terrible conditions at the Sham Shui Po and North Point Camps.

The Japanese also ignored a 1907 agreement not to use POWs for war-related work, and the Canadians at Hong Kong were put to work levelling a small mountain to expand Kai Tak airport. Nevertheless, the prisoners managed to sabotage the runway at least once without being caught. In 1942, the Japanese shipped POWs to Japan to work in mines, factories, and shipyards. By the time the war ended, of a total of 1,184 Canadians worked as slave labour in Japan, 136 had died of overwork on a meagre diet exacerbated by poor sanitation and lack of hygiene in primitive living conditions. Red Cross parcels were seldom distributed to the prisoners. After the war, liberators found warehouses full of parcels that had never been given out. From the Japanese point of view, to be taken prisoner was so shameful the prisoners were considered subhuman.

The only Canadian officer captured in Hong Kong who was taken to Japan was Major John Anthony Gibson Reid, a medical officer to the Winnipeg Grenadiers. In Japan he had to contend with short rations, no medicine, discouraging conditions, and worry about what the unpredictable Japanese would do next. He spent his own money to buy medical supplies for his patients. To his credit, he eventually managed to win the respect of the Japanese, and after the war he was recommended for a DSO, but, over protests from the Canadian authorities, the award was refused by the King's Awards Committee.

Getting to the Cemeteries and Memorials

> So what is left? I ask of the dawn wind
> As morning rises blue and bruised, like a boxer.
> What is left? I ask of the silence at the heart of the whirlwind,
> Ask of high Heaven, with its ragged, indifferent clouds.[16]

Captain Frank Pickersgill, Lieutenant Roméo Sabourin, Lieutenant Robert Byerly, Captain François Deniset, and Major Gustave Bieler of the SOE, who were imprisoned at Buchenwald Concentration Camp and later brutally executed, are memorialized on the **Groesbeek Memorial** (see p. 205)). A sixth Canadian SOE agent, Lieutenant Alcide Beauregard, was among 120 prisoners massacred by the Gestapo at Fort de la Côte Lorette on August 20, 1944. His name is inscribed on the **Bayeux Memorial** (see pp. 163). Ken Macalister's name is included among 135 names of SOE operatives serving with the British Forces who died at the hands of the Nazis and are memorialized on the **Brookwood Memorial** (see pp. 86).

Poznan Old Garrison Cemetery, in Poland, is the last resting place for 174 prisoners of World War I, airmen of World War II, and POWs from various camps in the area. Of the 283 Commonwealth World War II burials, 23 are Canadian, including the 6 murdered by the SS after the Great Escape. The other murdered POWs captured after the escape are also buried here.

By car: From Berlin, follow the signs for A113/E36, direction Leipzig/ Dresden/Frankfurt/Flughafen. Merge onto A113 and continue for 19 kilometres to the interchange 3-Schönefelder Kreuz. Keep right and follow the signs for A10/Berliner Ring toward Frankfurt (Oder). After 13 kilometres, keep right to follow A12 following signs for Warschau/ Warszawa/Frankfurt and continue for 59 kilometres. Cross into Poland

and continue on E30 for 164 kilometres. Take the exit for Armii Poznań and turn right on Armii Poznań to Dolna Wilna for 2 kilometres, then take the right fork onto Piatowska. Continue onto Droga Dębińska to Strzelecka, then Kazimierza Wielkiego. Turn left onto Mostowa, then left onto Wielka. Take the first right onto Garbary, and continue onto Aleja Armii Poznań. Poznan Old Garrison Cemetery is 500 metres on the right.

Kraków Rakowicki Cemetery holds Commonwealth burials brought in from Stalag VIII-B (later known as Stalag 344), from hospital grave-yards and airmen who lost their lives in the Warsaw supply drop and in bombing raids. In all, 483 Commonwealth casualties are buried here. Of the fifteen Canadians, 7 are RCAF airmen and 8 are infantrymen held as POWs.

By car: From Plac Jana Nowaka Jesiorańskiego in Krakow, Poland, head north on Pawia for eight hundred metres toward Stanislawa Worcella, and take the ramp to Aleja 29 Listopada. After eight hundred metres, turn right onto Biskopa Jana Prandoty. Kraków Rakowicki Cemetery is four hundred metres on the right. From the entrance, continue straight for one hundred metres, then turn left at the CWGC sign. The CWGC burials are on the western fringe of the larger cemetery.

Monument to World War II partizans,
Rakowicki Cemetery, Kraków, Poland.

Prague War Cemetery. (Commonwealth War Graves Commission)

Prague War Cemetery is located at the eastern fringe of Prague, in the Czech Republic, at the intersection of Vinohradská road leading from the city centre and Jana Želviského. The cemetery occupies the northwest corner of the eastern half of the large communal cemetery, which is divided by Jana Želviského. After the war, burials scattered around the country were brought in to be reburied in a single central cemetery. Of the 256 Commonwealth burials, many of whom died as prisoners of war, 9 are Canadian and 34 are unidentified.

Yokohama War Cemetery in Japan is located in the Hodogaya Ward, 9 kilometres from the city centre of Yokohama. It can be found in the same park area as the Botanical Gardens. Of the more than 1,500

Commonwealth burials, 137 are Canadian, all but 1—Lieutenant William Asbridge of the Royal Canadian Naval Reserve—soldiers of the Winnipeg Grenadiers and the Royal Rifles of Canada.

IN CANADA

The Halifax Memorial (Sailors' Memorial), Point Pleasant Park, Halifax, Nova Scotia

The Halifax Memorial was erected by the Commonwealth War Graves Commission to commemorate the Canadian sailors, merchant seamen, soldiers, and nursing sisters of both wars, who lost their lives at sea and also the names of men of the Canadian Army stationed in Canada who have no known grave. The names of 2,847 Canadian casualties of the Second World War are listed on panels four to twenty-three. Panels one to three list 272 Canadian naval casualties and 2 British casualties of World War I.

(Susan Evans Shaw)

IN CANADA

Ottawa, Ontario, The National Military Cemetery of the Canadian Forces, Beechwood Cemetery,

Between 2001 and 2007, the Beechwood Cemetery Foundation, in conjunction with the Commonwealth War Graves Commission, the Department of National Defence, and Veterans Affairs Canada, set aside sections of the Beechwood Cemetery in Ottawa to establish the National Military Cemetery. Funded in 1873 and designatfinal resting place for over 75,000 Canadians, including governors-general and prime ministers; the National Military Cemetery within its gates honours and brings together thousands of men and women who died in active service or who served honourably and chose to be interred among their comrades in our nation's capital.

(Susan Evans Shaw)

Acknowledgements

This project began as a natural follow-up to *Canadians at War: Vol. 1, A Guide to the Battlefields and Memorials of World War I*. Some schools of historical thought consider the two world wars of the twentieth century as a single war with a twenty-one year-interlude. It therefore seemed inevitable that my thoughts should turn to the second world war almost as soon as the first volume launched. I wasn't alone in my thinking, and on a visit to the Goose Lane offices in Fredericton, publisher Susanne Alexander straightaway asked if I was interested in following up with a similar volume on World War II.

Once again, in terms of knowledge I had to start almost from scratch. My high school history classes on the two world wars were but a dim memory, especially as at the time I knew my grades were high enough that I would be excused final exams, thus freeing me from the onerous chore of memorizing names, dates, and events. To make up for my past dilatory studies, I needed to do a lot of reading. My preference has always been to have my own books for referral and to annotate. For what I couldn't find on their shelves, Bryan Prince Bookseller never let me down on special orders. I also found excellent resources in used books at Hamilton's J.H. Gordon Books and Westdale Bookworm.

Fellow author Gillian Chan gave me invaluable advice and the loan of an excellent book on the fall of Hong Kong. On the subject of Hong Kong, a huge thank you to my nephew, Peter Dostal, and his wife, Kate Hopfner, who took time out of a holiday to photograph sites in Hong Kong.

Again my thanks to David Bartlett and Chris Wesley of Bartlett's Battlefield Journeys for organizing as comprehensive a tour of Normandy as time allowed. Special thanks to Chris for the loan of his camera for a day when I mislaid the spare battery for my own camera.

Beverly Bayzat and the staff of the William Ready Archives and Research Collections at McMaster University are again responsible for the scans of maps from the three volumes of the *Official History of the Canadians in the Second World War*. Susan Ross of the Canadian War Museum supplied the images taken of the Sherman tank and DUKW tank chosen from their wide-ranging collection of military equipment in the LeBreton Gallery.

Newfoundland dogs are an uncommon breed, and I for one wanted an image to stand in for Sergeant Gander as quality contemporary photos of him are almost impossible to come by. Donavon and June Porter of Haileybury, Ontario, kindly photographed Rufus and provided his height and weight to illustrate Sergeant Gander's impressive size. Thank you to Peterborough poet Betsy Struthers for putting me in touch with her brother.

As always, friends and family had a role to play. Tony and Lynne Nutkins were again travel companions, this time to Normandy, and Tony kindly provided photographs of Dieppe. My niece Alix Dostal braved Ottawa's bitter March winds to photograph the statue of William Lyon Mackenzie King on Parliament Hill from every angle so I would have a selection from which to choose. Janice Jackson provided the stunning cover photo of the Juno Beach Centre sculpture, *Remembrance and Renewal,* and the charming image on the cover of the slope-shouldered veteran watching from the curb at a Warrior's Day Parade.

Military history can be highly technical and full of jargon so I owe a vote of thanks to my creative writing colleagues of the Canadian Federation of University Women, Linda Helson, Jean Rae Baxter, Debbie Welland, Alexandra Gall, Barbara Ledger, and Cathy Spencer, who critiqued various chapters and made suggestions to keep the account of events of the World War II intelligible to the general reader.

Editors Barry Norris and Charles Stuart helped me polish the manuscript, providing invaluable insight and advice at the final stages of preparation. At Goose Lane Editions, Martin Ainsley, with humour and empathy, kept our collective noses to the grindstone in order to meet a very tight deadline, while Julie Scriver had the difficult task of preparing the maps and a very mixed assortment of photos to illustrate the text. I cannot thank them all enough.

As I mentioned at the beginning, the whole undertaking necessitated intensive study, which I pursue to this day. Nevertheless, mistakes happen. Any errors are my own.

Illustration Credits

Full illustration credits appear with the images. All illustrations are reproduced with permission or are in the public domain. Photographs used under Creative Commons licenses are so noted in the credit lines. URLs for the licenses indicated are as follows:

Notes

Please note: Historical information for the cemeteries described in this book comes from the website of the Commonwealth War Graves Commission, www.cwgc.org. Cemetery details may be accessed by putting the name of the cemetery into the search box at: http://www.cwgc.org/debt_of_honour.asp?meniud=14&searchFor=cemetery.

Preface

1   Jonathan Vance, *Unlikely Soldiers: How Two Canadians Fought the Secret War Against Nazi Occupation* (Toronto: HarperCollins Publishers Limited, 2008), 259.

2   Michael Ignatieff, *True Patriot Love: Four Generations in Search of Canada* (Toronto: Penguin Books Limited, 2009), 135.

Introduction

1   C.P. Stacey, *Six Years of War: The Army in Canada, Britain and the Pacific*, vol. 1, *Official History of the Canadians in the Second World War* (Ottawa: The Queen's Printer, 1966), 3.

2   Ibid, 4.

3   Tim Cook, *The Madman and the Butcher: The Sensational Wars of Sam Hughes and General Arthur Currie* (Toronto: Allen Lane Canada, 2010), 285.

4   Tim Cook, *Shock Troops: Canadians Fighting the Great War 1917-1918 Volume Two* (Toronto: Viking Canada, 2008), 632.

5   Daniel Dancocks, *Sir Arthur Currie: A Biography* (Toronto: Methuen, 1985), 205. "When the war ended, the British government generously rewarded its top soldiers: Sir Douglas Haig was given £100,000 and an earldom, Sir John French and Sir Edmund Allenby both received £50,000, while army commanders were given a grant of £30,000 each and corps commanders £10,000 each.

6   Brock died six weeks later at the family farm in Strathroy, Ontario.

7   Dancocks, *Sir Arthur Currie*, 280-2.

8   Robert J. Sharpe, *The Last Day, the Last Hour: The Currie Libel Trial* (Toronto: The Osgoode Society, 1988), 246.

9   C.P. Stacey, "The Divine Mission: Mackenzie King and Hitler." *Canadian Historical Review* 61 (1980): 502-12.

10   Stacey, *Six Years of War*, 3.

11   Cook, *Shock Troops*, 611.

12   J.W. Pickersgill, *Seeing Canada Whole: A Memoir* (Toronto: Fitzhenry & Whiteside, 1994), 149.

13   Antony Beevor, *The Second World War* (New York: Little, Brown and Company Hachette Book Group, 2012), 4.

14   Ian Kershaw, *Hitler: 1936-1945 Nemesis* (London: Penguin Books, 2001), 78-9.

15   J.W. Pickersgill, *Seeing Canada Whole,* 170.

16   Ibid., 172.

17   The lone dissenting voice was that of J.S. Woodsworth, who spoke not for his party, the Co-operative Commonwealth Federation (CCF), but for himself as a lifelong conscientious pacifist. His speech was received with a respectful silence that gave hope of domestic harmony, unlike the bitterness of the 1917 Conscription Crisis.

PART I: The Eve of War

1   John Nelson Rickard, *The Politics of Command: Lieutenant-General A.G.M. McNaughton and the Canadian Army 1939-1943* (Toronto: University of Toronto Press Inc., 2010), 40.

2   Stacey, *Six Years of War*, 35.

3   Ibid., 48.

4   Ibid., 80.

5   David J. Bercuson, *Maple Leaf Against the Axis: Canada's Second World War* (Toronto: Stoddart Publishing Co. Ltd., 1995), 273.

6   Richard Malone, *A Portrait of War: 1939-1943* (Toronto: Collins Publishers, 1983), 24-5.

7   Rickard, *Politics of Command*, 119-20.

8   Stacy, *Six Years of War*, 415.

9   J.L. Granatstein, *The Generals: The Canadian Army's Senior Commanders in the Second World War* (Toronto: Stoddart Publishing Co. Ltd., 1993), 33.

10   Farley Mowat, *The Regiment* (Toronto: McClelland and Stewart Limited, 1955), 23.

11   John Swettenham, *McNaughton: Volume 2, 1939-1943* (Toronto: The Ryerson Press, 1969), 12.

12   Mowat, *Regiment*, 26.

13   Swettenham, *McNaughton,* 151.

14   Terry Copp, *Fields of Fire*: *The Canadians in Normandy.* (Toronto: University of Toronto Press Incorporated, 1998),17-8.

15   Stacey, *Six Years of War*, 243.

16   Rickard, *Politics of Command,* 40.

17   Stacey, *Six Years of War*, 280.

18   Rickard, *Politics of Command*, 41.

19   Swettenham, *McNaughton*, 106-7.

20   Mowat, *The Regiment*, 35.

21   Stacey, *Six Years of War,* 271.

22   Swettenham, *McNaughton*, 91-2.

23   Ibid., 57.

24   Beevor, *Second World War*, 136.

25   Bercuson, *Maple Leaf Against the Axis*, 32.

26   Beevor, *Second World War*, 137.

27   Stacey, *Six Years of War*, 88.

28   Ibid., 413.

29   Website of the Commonwealth War Graves Commission: www.cwgc.org.

PART II: The Canadians in Hong Kong

1   John A. English, *Failure in High Command: The Canadian Army and the Normandy Campaign* (Ottawa: The Golden Dog Press. 1995), 108.

2   Philip Snow, *The Fall of Hong Kong: Britain, China and the Japanese Occupation* (New Haven, CT: Yale University Press, 2004), 36-7.

3   William Manchester and Paul Reid, *The Last Lion; Winston Spencer Churchill Defender of the Realm 1940-1965* (New York: Little, Brown and Company, 2012), 402.

4   Stacey, *Six Years of War*, 440-1.

5   Ibid., 447.

6   Robyn Walker, *Sergeant Gander: A Canadian Hero* (Toronto: Natural Heritage Books, 2009), 49.

7   Beevor, *Second World War,* 259-60.

8   Walker, *Sergeant Gander*, 66.

9   Ko Tim Keung and Jason Wordie, *Ruins of War: A Guide to Hong Kong's Battlefields and Wartime Sites* (Hong Kong: Joint Publishing [H.K.] Co. Ltd., 1995), 97.

10   Snow, *Fall of Hong Kong,* 80-1.

11   Stacey, *Six Years of War*, 488.

12   Ibid., 488.

13   Ibid., 491.

14   Driving directions are from Google Maps. Transit directions are from Google Maps with the help of *Ruins of War: A Guide to Hong Kong's Battlefield and Wartime Sites* by Ko Tim Keumg and Jason Wordie.

PART III: Crossing from England to Northwest Europe

1   Thomas D'Arcy McGee, "Jacques Cartier," *Canadian Ballads, and Occasional Verses* (Montreal, 1858), 11.

2   Morris Bishop, *Champlain: The Life of Fortitude* (London: MacDonald & Co. [Publishers] Ltd., 1949), 9.

3   Ibid., 42.

4   R. Allen Brown, *Dover Castle Ministry of Public Building and Works OFFICIAL GUIDEBOOK* (London: Her Majesty's Stationary Office, 1966), 45.

5   Stacey, *Six Years of War*, 399.

6 Nathan M. Greenfield, "Deconstructing Dieppe." *The Walrus* 9, no. 7 (September 2012), 42.

7 Denis Whitaker and Shelagh Whitaker, *Dieppe: Tragedy to Triumph,* (Whitby, ON: McGraw-Hill Ryerson Limited, 1992), 73.

8 Whitaker and Whitaker, *Dieppe,* 72.

9 Ibid., 87.

10 Philip Ziegler, *Mountbatten: A Biography* (New York: Alfred A. Knopf, 1985), 189.

11 Whitaker and Whitaker, *Dieppe*, 125.

12 Stacey, *Six Years of War,* 349.

13 Letter to his parents and sister from Private George Kerslake of the RHLI written 18/8/42. Private Kerslake did not survive the attack at Dieppe.

14 Stacey, *Six Years of War*, 345.

15 Ibid., 362.

16 Ibid., 370.

17 Greenfield, "Deconstructing Dieppe," 41-9.

18 Whitaker and Whitaker, *Dieppe*, 249.

19 Ibid., 253.

20 D.J. Goodspeed, *Battle Royal: A History of the Royal Regiment of Canada 1862-1962* (Toronto: Charters Publishing Co. Ltd., 1962), 400-1.

21 Whitaker and Whitaker, *Dieppe*, 267-8.

22 Ibid.. 269.

23 Ibid., 271.

24 Winston S. Churchill, "The Hinge of Fate," in *The Second World War, Volume 4* (Boston: Houghton Mifflin Co., 1950), 510.

25 Philip Ziegler, *Mountbatten*, 189.

26 Ibid., 196.

27 Stacey, *Six Years of War*, 393-4; Swettenham, *McNaughton*, 249.

28 The DSO is awarded for meritorious or distinguished service by officers of the armed forces during wartime, typically in actual combat.

29 Bercuson, *Maple Leaf Against the Axis*, 74.

30 Manchester and Reid, *Last Lion,* 568.

Part IV: The Canadians in Italy

1 Duncan Fraser, "Italian Countryside Site of War That Never Was," Halifax *Herald* Limited, quoted in Daniel Dancocks, *The D-Day Dodgers: The Canadians in Italy, 1943-45* (Toronto: McClelland & Stewart Inc., 1991), 438.

2 Ibid., 7.

3 Ibid., 18.

4 Ibid., 9.

5 G.W.L. Nicholson, *The Canadians in Italy 1943-1945*, vol. 2, *Official History of the Canadians in the Second World War* (Ottawa: The Queen's Printer, 1956, 19.

6   Ibid., 20.
7   Ibid, 26.
8   Dancocks, *D-Day Dodgers*, 24.
9   Dominick Graham, *The Price of Command: A Biography of General Guy Simonds* (Toronto: Stoddart Publishing Co. Ltd., 1993), 78.
10 Beevor, *Second World War*, 497.
11 Mowat, *Regiment*, 82-92; Dancocks. *D-Day Dodgers*, 62.
12 A reference to the sleeve patch worn by the Canadians. Battle dress for all Allied troops was the same khaki.
13 Nicholson, *Canadians in Italy*, 141.
14 Dancocks, *D-Day Dodgers*, 96.
15 Nicholson, *Canadians in Italy,* 176.
16 Beevor, *Second World War*, 496.
17 Dancocks, *D-Day Dodgers*, 87.
18 Ibid., 103.
19 Puzzled why Lieutenant Stewart should be buried at Agira when his unit was not serving in Sicily, the author instituted an investigation by Library and Archives Canada. Lieutenant Stewart was not serving with the Canadian Black Watch but with the British Black Watch (Royal Highland Regiment) which was serving in Sicily at the time. A note has been sent to the CWGC to correct the error. The LAC database will also be corrected.
20 CWGC website: www.cwgc.org.
21 Mowat, *Regiment*, 107.
22 Dancocks, *D-Day Dodgers*, 118.
23 Malone, *Portrait of War*, 176.
24 Dancocks, *D-Day Dodgers*, 114.
25 Ibid., 121.
26 Ibid., 124.
27 Ibid.
28 CWGC website: www.cwgc.org.
29 Mark Zuehlke, *Ortona: Canada's Epic World War II Battle* (Toronto: Stoddart Publishing Co. Ltd., 1999), 10-1.
30 Dancocks, *D-Day Dodgers*, 139.
31 Ibid., 143-4.
32 Zuehlke, *Oronta*, 52.
33 Ibid., 44-5.
34 Nicholson, *Canadians in Italy*, 339.
35 Dancocks, *D-Day Dodgers*, 181.
36 Richard Malone *Portrait of War,* 225.
37 Nicholson, *Canadians in Italy*, 338.
38 Dancocks, *D-Day Dodgers*, 214.
39 Ibid., 220.

40   Nicholson, *Canadians in Italy*, 374.

41   Dancocks. *D-Day Dodgers*, 223.

42   Ibid., 229.

43   Nicholson, *Canadians in Italy*, 394.

44   Dancocks, *D-Day Dodgers*, 236.

45   Ibid., 286.

46   Nicholson, *Canadians in Italy*, 452.

47   CWGC website: www.cwgc.org.

48   Dancocks, *D-Day Dodgers,* 296.

49   Nicholson, *Canadians in Italy*, 470-2.

50   Dancocks, *D-Day Dodgers*, 296.

51   CWGC website: www.cwgc.org.

52   Nicholson, *Canadians in Italy*, 507.

53   Dancocks, *D-Day Dodgers*, 326.

54   Ibid., 345.

55   Nicholson, *Italian Campaign*, 473.

56   Kershaw, *Hitler,* 717.

57   Princess Louise was just a foal whose mother had been killed when the 8th Hussars found her. She remained the Regimental mascot until her death in 1973.

58   Lloyd Oliver, one of the truckers, found the youngster and he and the other truckers adopted him. They made him "Corporal," providing him with his own uniform. An officer thwarted the attempt to smuggle him out of Italy and Oliver delivered the boy to a foster family in Ravenna. In 1980, Oliver located Gino and arranged a reunion with fifteen of the truckers at his farm in Miniota, Manitoba. The farm had previously belonged to the author's great-uncle and aunt, Jack and Gwladys Taylor. Dancocks, *D-Day Dodgers*, 419.

59   Ibid., 418.

60   Ibid., 270.

61   CWGC website: www.cwgc.org.

PART V: The Canadians in Northwest Europe

1   Beevor, *Second World War*, 571.

2   Copp, *Fields of Fire*, 19.

3   Colonel C.P. Stacey, *The Victory Campaign: The Operations in North-West Europe 1944-1945, vol. 3 (Official History of the Canadians in the Second World War,* (Ottawa: The Queen's Printer, 1966), 48-9.

4   Ibid., 51.

5   Copp, *Fields of Fire,* 37.

6   Beevor, *Second World War*, 574.

7   Arthur Bryant, *Triumph in the West, 1943-1946* (London: Collins Clear Type Press, 1959), 200.

8   Stacey, *Victory Campaign*, 72.

9   Copp, *Fields of Fire*, 21.

10   King Whyte, *Letters Home 1944-1946* (Canada: Seraphim Editions, 2007), 15.

11   Copp, *Fields of Fire*, 14-5.

12   Stacey, *Victory Campaign*, 91.

13   Ibid., 117.

14   Copp, *Fields of Fire,* 41.

15   Denis Whitaker and Shelagh Whitaker with Terry Copp, *Victory at Falaise: The Soldiers' Story: The Defeat of the German Army in Normandy August 1944* (Toronto: HarperCollins Publishers Ltd., 2000), 13.

16   Copp, *Fields of Fire*, 65.

17   Bercuson, *Maple Leaf Against the Axis,* 212.

18   Copp, *Fields of Fire,* 66-7.

19   Ibid., 75-6.

20   Stacey, *Victory Campaign*, 141.

21   Nigel Hamilton, *Master of the Battlefield: Monty's War Years 1942-1944* (New York: McGraw-Hill Book Company, 1983), 715.

22   Stacey, *Victory Campaign*, 155.

23   Graham, *Price of Command*, 126.

24   Copp, *Fields of Fire*, 109-10.

25   Ibid., 135.

26   Ibid., 148.

27   Hamilton, *Master of the Battlefield*, 754.

28   Stacey, *Victory Campaign*, 191.

29   Graham, *Price of Command*, 146.

30   Copp, *Fields of Fire*, 170.

31   Ibid., 169-71.

32   Malone, *World in Flames,* 62.

33   "Priests" were 105 mm self-propelled guns. "Unfrocked Priests" were Priests with the guns and screens for gunners removed to become armoured personnel carriers; they were soon designated "Kangaroos."

34   Copp, *Fields of Fire*, 198.

35   Stacey, *Victory Campaign*, 229.

36   Copp, *Fields of Fire*, 218.

37   Stacey, *Victory Campaign*, 270.

38   Ibid., 228.

39   Ibid., 277.

40   Manchester and Reid, *Last Lion*, 854.

41   Stacey, *Victory Campaign*, 282.

42   Ibid., 323-4.

43   Ibid., 301.

44   Ibid.

45   Ibid., 316.
46   Michael Clark, "Cinderella Army: The Canadians in North-West Europe 1944-1945"
     by Terry Copp. Review in *Quill and Quire*, September 2006.
47   Denis Whitaker and Shelagh Whitaker, *Tug of War: The Canadian Victory that
     Opened Antwerp* (Toronto: Stoddart Publishing Co. Ltd.. 1984), 307-8.
48   Ibid., 263-4.
49   Terry Copp, *Cinderella Army: The Canadians in Northwest Europe 1944-1945*
     (Toronto: University of Toronto Press, 2006), 116.
50   Ibid., 117.
51   Stacey, *Victory Campaign*, 400.
52   Ibid., 383-91.
53   Copp, *Cinderella Army*, 166.
54   Ibid., 169-70.
55   Whitaker and Whitaker, *Tug of War*, 212.
56   Ibid., 216.
57   Copp, *Cinderella Army,* 179.
58   Whitaker and Whitaker, *Tug of War*, 35.
59   Copp, *Cinderella Army*, 244.
60   Stacey, *Victory Campaign*, 471.
61   Ibid., 498-501.
62   Ibid., 511.
63   Copp, *Cinderella Army*, 243.
64   Ibid., 200.
65   Ibid., Stacey, 529.
66   Ibid., 530.
67   Ibid., 537.
68   Copp, *Cinderella Army*, 257.
69   Ibid., 263-4.
70   Stacey, *Victory Campaign,* 587.

PART VI: Last Things
1   Stacey, *Six Years of War*, 297.
2   Ibid., 299.
3   Ibid., 305-6.
4   Ibid., 207-10.
5   John Bryden, *Deadly Allies: Canada's Secret War 1939-1947* (Toronto: McClelland &
    Stewart Inc., 1989), 34.
6   Ibid., 34-8.
7   Ibid., 61.
8   Ibid., 256.

9   Daniel Dancocks, *In Enemy Hands: Canadian Prisoners of War* (Edmonton: Hurtig Publishers Ltd., 1983), ix.

10   Ibid., 1-2.

11   John Mellor, *Dieppe—Canada's Forgotten Heroes* (Toronto: Methuen Publications. First Signet Printing, 1979), 117.

12   Jonathan Vance, *Objects of Concern: Canadian Prisoners of War Through the Twentieth Century* (Vancouver: UBC Press, 1994), 135.

13   Dancocks, *In Enemy Hands*, x.

14   Mellor, *Dieppe—Canada's Forgotten Heroes*, 191-2.

15   Dancocks, *In Enemy Hands*, 188-219.

16   Douglas LePan, *Macalister, or Dying in the Dark* [excerpt] (Kingston: Quarry Press Inc., 1995), 91.

Selected Bibliography

Barris, Ted. *Days of Victory: Canadians Remember, 1939-1945 Sixtieth Anniversary Edition.* Toronto: Thomas Allen Publications, 2005.

Beevor, Antony. *The Second World War.* New York: Little, Brown and Company Hachette Book Group, 2012.

Bercuson, David J. *Maple Leaf Against the Axis: Canada's Second World War.* Toronto: Stoddart Publishing Co. Ltd., 1995.

_____ and S.F. Wise, eds. *The Valour and the Horror Revisited.* Montreal & Kingston: McGill-Queen's University Press, 1994.

Bishop, Morris. *Champlain: The Life of Fortitude.* London: MacDonald & Co. (Publishers) Ltd., 1949.

Brown, R. Allen. *Dover Castle: Ministry of Public Building and Works OFFICIAL GUIDEBOOK.* London: Her Majesty's Stationary Office, 1966.

Bryant, Sir Arthur. *Triumph in the West, 1943-1946: Based on the Diaries and Autobiographical Notes of Field Marshal The Viscount Alanbrooke.* (London: Collins Clear Type Press, 1959.

Bryden, John. *Deadly Allies: Canada's Secret War 1937-1947.* Toronto: McClelland & Stewart Inc., 1989.

Cook, Tim. *The Madman and the Butcher: The Sensational Wars of Sam Hughes and General Arthur Currie.* Toronto: Allen Lane Canada, 2010.

_____. *Shock Troops: Canadians Fighting the Great War 1917-1918 Volume Two.* Toronto: Viking Canada, 2008.

Copp, Terry. *Cinderella Army: The Canadians in Northwest Europe 1944-1945.* Toronto: University of Toronto Press, 2006.

_____. *Fields of Fire: The Canadians in Normandy.* Toronto: University of Toronto Press Incorporated, 1998.

Dancocks, Daniel G. *The D-Day Dodgers: The Canadians in Italy, 1943-1945.* Toronto: McClelland & Stewart Inc., 1991.

_____. *In Enemy Hands: Canadian Prisoners of War 1939-1945.* Edmonton: Hurtig Publishers Ltd., 1983.

_____. *Sir Arthur Currie: A Biography.* Toronto: Methuen, 1985.

Dunn, Hunter. *Memoirs of a WWII Armoured Officer.* Hunter Dunn, 2005.

English, John A. *Failure in High Command: The Canadian Army and the Normandy Campaign.* Ottawa: The Golden Dog Press, 1995.

Gillies, Midge. *The Barbed-Wire University: The Real Lives of Allied Prisoners of War in the Second World War.* London: Aurum Press Ltd., 2012.

Goodspeed, D.J. *Battle Royal: A History of the Royal Regiment of Canada 1862-1962*. Toronto: Charters Publishing Company Limited, 1962.

Graham, Dominick. *The Price of Command: A Biography of General Guy Simonds*. Toronto: Stoddart Publishing Co. Ltd., 1993.

Granatstein, J.L. *The Generals: The Canadian Army's Senior Commanders in the Second World War*. Toronto: Stoddart Publishing Co. Limited, 1993.

Greenfield, Nathan M. "Deconstructing Dieppe" in *The Walrus*, Vol. 9, No. 7, September 2012.

Hamilton, Nigel. *Master of the Battlefield: Monty's War Years 1942-1944*. New York: McGraw-Hill Book Company, 1983.

_____. *Monty: Final Years of the Field Marshall 1944-1976*. New York: McGraw-Hill Book Company, 1986.

Ignatieff, Michael. *True Patriot Love: Four Generations in Search of Canada*. Toronto: Viking Canada, 2009.

Keegan, John. *The Battle for History: Re-Fighting World War Two*. The Barbara Frum Lectureship. Toronto: Vintage Books, a division of Random House of Canada Limited, 1995.

_____. *The Face of Battle*. New York: The Viking Press, 1976.

Kershaw, Ian. *Hitler: 1936-1945 Nemesis*. London: Penguin Books, 2001.

Keung, Ko Tim and Jason Wordie. *Ruins of War: A Guide to Hong Kong's Battlefields and Wartime Sites*. Hong Kong: Joint Publishing (H.K.) Co. Ltd., 1996.

LePan, Douglas. *Macalister, or Dying in the Dark*. Kingston: Quarry Press Inc., 1995.

Malone, Richard. *A Portrait of War 1939-1943*. Toronto: Collins Publishers, 1983.

_____. *A World in Flames 1944-1945: A Portrait of War: Part Two*. Toronto: Collins Publishers, 1984.

Manchester, William. *The Last Lion: Winston Spencer Churchill Alone 1932-1940*. New York: Bantam Doubleday Dell Publishing Group Inc., 1989.

_____ and Paul Reid. *The Last Lion: Winston Spencer Churchill Defender of the Realm 1940-1965*. New York: Little, Brown and Company, 2012.

Mellor, John. *Dieppe—Canada's Forgotten Heroes*. Toronto: Methuen Publications. First Signet Printing, 1979.

Monsarrat, Nicholas. *The Cruel Sea*. Toronto: Penguin Books (Canada), 2009.

Mowat, Farley. *And No Birds Sang*. Vancouver: Douglas & McIntyre, 2012.

_____. *The Regiment*. Toronto: McClelland and Stewart Limited, 1973.

Nicholson, G.W.L. *The Canadians in Italy 1943-1945*. Ottawa: The Queen's Printer, 1966. (Official History of the Canadians in the Second World War, Volume II).

Pickersgill, Frank. *The Making of a Secret Agent*. Edited by George H. Ford. Halifax: Goodread Biographies, James Lorimer, 1983.

_____. *The Pickersgill Letters: Written by Frank Pickersgill During the Period 1934-1943 and edited with a Memoir by George H. Ford*. Toronto: The Ryerson Press, 1948.

Pickersgill, J.W. *Seeing Canada Whole: A Memoir*. Toronto: Fitzhenry & Whiteside, 1994.

Rickard, John Nelson. *The Politics of Command: Lieutenant General A.G.L. McNaughton* and the Canadian Army 1939-1943. Toronto: University of Toronto Press Incorporated, 2010.

Sharpe, Robert L. The Last Day, The Last Hour: The Currie Libel Trial. Toronto: The Osgood Society, 1988.

Snow, Philip. The Fall of Hong Kong: Britain, China and the Japanese Occupation. New Haven and London: Yale University Press, 2004.

Stacey, C.P. "The Divine Mission: Mackenzie King and Hitler." Canadian Historical Review, LXI, 4, 1980.

_____. Six Years of War: The Army in Canada, Britain and the Pacific. Ottawa: The Queen's Printer, 1966. (Official History of the Canadians in the Second World War, Volume I).

_____. The Victory Campaign: The Operations in North-West Europe 1944-1945. Ottawa: The Queen's Printer, 1966. (Official History of the Canadians in the Second World War, Volume III).

Swettenham, John. McNaughton Volume Two 1939-1943. Toronto: The Ryerson Press, 1969.

Vance, Jonathan F. Objects of Concern: Canadian Prisoners of War Through the Twentieth Century. Vancouver: UBC Press, 1994.

_____. Unlikely Soldiers: How Two Canadians Fought the Secret War Against the Nazi Occupation. Toronto: HarperCollins Publishers Ltd., 2008.

Walker, Robyn. Sergeant Gander: A Canadian Hero. Toronto: Natural Heritage Books, A Member of the Dundurn Group, 2009.

Whitaker, Denis, and Shelagh Whitaker. Dieppe: Tragedy to Triumph. Whitby, Ontario: McGraw-Hill Ryerson Limited, 1992.

_____. Tug of War: The Canadian Victory that Opened Antwerp. Toronto: Stoddart Publishing Co. Limited. 1984.

Whitaker, Denis, and Shelagh Whitaker with Terry Copp. Victory at Falaise: The Soldiers' Story: The Defeat of the German Army in Normandy August 1944. Toronto: HarperCollins Publishers Ltd., 2000.

Whyte, King. Letters Home 1944-1946. Canada: Seraphim Editions, 2007.

Ziegler, Philip. Mountbatten: A Biography. New York: Alfred A. Knopf, 1985.

Zuehkle, Mark. Ortona: Canada's Epic World War II Battle. Toronto: Stoddart Publishing Co. Limited, 1999.

Index

Please note: All Army units are listed by country of origin. All cemeteries and memorials are listed by category and individually. All battles, medals. operations, prisoner-of-war camps, Resistance groups, and weapons are listed by category.